Lecture Notes in
Microeconomic Theory

Lecture Notes in Microeconomic Theory

The Economic Agent

Second Edition

Ariel Rubinstein

PRINCETON UNIVERSITY PRESS

PRINCETON AND OXFORD

Published by Princeton University Press, 41 William Street, Princeton,
New Jersey 08540

In the United Kingdom: Princeton University Press, 60 Oxford Street,
Woodstock, Oxfordshire OX20 1TW

press.princeton.edu

Library of Congress Cataloging-in-Publication Data

Rubinstein, Ariel.
  Lecture notes in microeconomic theory : the economic agent /
  Ariel Rubinstein. – 2nd ed.
    p. cm.
  Includes bibliographical references and index.
  ISBN 978-0-691-15413-8 (pbk. : alk. paper)
    1. Microeconomics.   2. Economics.   I. Title.

 HB172.R72 2011
 338.5–dc23

                                              2011026862

British Library Cataloging-in-Publication Data is available

This book has been composed in Times.

Printed on acid-free paper. ∞

Typeset by S R Nova Pvt Ltd, Bangalore, India

Printed in the United States of America

10 9 8 7 6 5 4 3 2 1

Contents

Preface

This is the second edition of my lecture notes for the first quarter of a microeconomics course for PhD (or MA) economics students. The lecture notes were developed over a period of 20 years during which I taught the course at Tel Aviv, Princeton, and New York universities.

I published the book for the first time in 2007 with some hesitation since several superb books were already on the shelves. Foremost among them is Kreps (1990), which pioneered the shift of the game theoretic revolution from research papers into textbooks. His book covers the material in depth and includes many ideas for future research. Mas-Colell, Whinston, and Green (1995) continued this trend with a very comprehensive and detailed textbook. There are three other books on my short list: Bowles (2003), which brings economics back to its authentic political economics roots; Jehle and Reny (1997), with its very precise style; and the classic Varian (1984). These five books constitute an impressive collection of textbooks for the standard advanced microeconomics course. My book covers only the first quarter of the standard course. It does not aim to compete with these books, but rather to supplement them. I published it only because I think that some of the didactic ideas presented might be beneficial to both students and teachers, and it is to this end that I insisted on retaining its lecture notes style.

Downloading Updated Versions
The book is posted on the Internet, and access is entirely free. I am grateful to Princeton University Press for allowing it to be downloaded for free right after publication. Since 2007, I have updated the book annually, adding material and correcting mistakes. My plan is to continue revising the book annually. To access the latest electronic version go to: http://arielrubinstein.tau.ac.il.

Solution Manual
Teachers of the course can also get an updated solution manual. I do my best to send the manual only to teachers of a graduate course in microeconomics. Requests for the manual should be made at: http://gametheory.tau.ac.il/microtheory.

Gender

Throughout the book I use only male pronouns. This is my deliberate choice and does not reflect the policy of the editors or the publishers. I believe that continuous reminders of the he/she issue simply divert readers' attention. Language is of course very important in shaping our thinking, and I don't dispute the importance of the type of language we use. But I feel it is more effective to raise the issue of discrimination against women in the discussion of gender-related issues rather than raising flags on every page of a book on economic theory.

Acknowledgments

I would like to thank all my teaching assistants, who made helpful comments during the many years I taught the course: Rani Spiegler, Kfir Eliaz, Yoram Hamo, Gabi Gayer, and Tamir Tshuva at Tel Aviv University; Bilge Yilmaz, Ronny Razin, Wojciech Olszewski, Attila Ambrus, Andrea Wilson, Haluk Ergin, and Daisuke Nakajima at Princeton; and Sophie Bade and Anna Ingster at NYU. Sharon Simmer and Rafi Aviav helped me with the English editing. Avner Shlain prepared the index. Special thanks to Rafi Aviav and Benjamin Bachi for their devoted work in producing the revised versions of the book.

Introduction

As a new graduate student, you are at the beginning of a new stage of your life. In a few months you will be overloaded with definitions, concepts, and models. Your teachers will be guiding you into the wonders of economics and will rarely have the time to stop to raise fundamental questions about what these models are supposed to mean. It is not unlikely that you will be brainwashed by the professional-sounding language and hidden assumptions. I am afraid I am about to initiate you into this inevitable process. Still, I want to use this opportunity to pause for a moment and alert you to the fact that many economists have strong and conflicting views about what economic theory is. Some see it as a *set of theories* that can (or should) be tested. Others see it as a *bag of tools* to be used by economic agents. Many see it as a *framework* through which professional and academic economists view the world.

My own view may disappoint those of you who have come to this course with practical motivations. In my view, economic theory is no more than an arena for the *investigation of concepts* we use in thinking about economics in real life. What makes a theoretical model "economics" is that the concepts we are analyzing are taken from real-life reasoning about economic issues. Through the investigation of these concepts, we indeed try to understand reality better, and the models provide a language that enables us to think about economic interactions in a systematic way. But I do not view economic models as an attempt to describe the world or to provide tools for predicting the future. I object to looking for an ultimate truth in economic theory, and I do not expect it to be the foundation for any policy recommendation. Nothing is "holy" in economic theory and everything is the creation of people like yourself.

Basically, this course is about a certain class of economic *concepts* and *models*. Although we will be studying formal concepts and models, they will always be given an interpretation. An economic model differs substantially from a purely mathematical model in that it is a *combination* of a mathematical model and its *interpretation*. The names of the mathematical objects are an integral part of an economic model. When mathematicians use terms such as "field" or "ring" that are in everyday use, it is only for the sake of convenience. When they name a collection of sets a "filter", they are doing so in an associative manner; in principle, they could call it "ice cream cone". When they use the term "good ordering", they are not making an ethical judgment. In contrast to mathematics, interpretation is an essential ingredient of any economic model.

The word "model" sounds more scientific than "fable" or "fairy tale", but I don't see much difference between them. The author of a fable draws a parallel to a situation in real life and has some moral he wishes to impart to the reader. The fable is an imaginary situation that is somewhere between fantasy and reality. Any fable can be dismissed as being unrealistic or simplistic, but this is also the fable's advantage. Being something between fantasy and reality, a fable is free of extraneous details and annoying diversions. In this unencumbered state, we can clearly discern what cannot always be seen from the real world. On our return to reality, we are in possession of some sound advice or a relevant argument that can be used in the real world. We do exactly the same thing in economic theory. Thus, a good model in economic theory, like a good fable, identifies a number of themes and elucidates them. We perform thought exercises that are only loosely connected to reality and have been stripped of most of their real-life characteristics. However, in a good model, as in a good fable, something significant remains. One can think about this book as an attempt to introduce the characters that inhabit economic fables. Here, we observe the characters in isolation. In models of markets and games, we further investigate the interactions between the characters.

It is my hope that some of you will react and attempt to change what is currently called economic theory and that you will acquire alternative ways of thinking about economic and social interactions. At the very least, this course should teach you to ask hard questions about economic models and the sense in which they are relevant to real-life economics. I hope that you walk away from this course with the recognition that the answers are not as obvious as they might appear.

Microeconomics

In this course we deal only with microeconomics, a collection of models in which the primitives are details about the behavior of units called *economic agents*. Microeconomic models investigate assumptions about economic agents' activities and about interactions between these agents. An economic agent is the basic unit operating in the model. When we construct a model with a particular economic scenario in mind, we might have some degree of freedom regarding whom we take to be the economic agents. Most often, we do have in mind that the economic agent is an individual, a person with one head, one heart, two eyes, and two ears. However, in some economic models, an economic agent is taken to be a nation, a family, or a parliament. At other times, the "individual" is broken down into a collection of economic agents, each operating in distinct circumstances, and each regarded as an economic agent.

We should not be too cheerful about the statement that an economic agent in microeconomics is not constrained to being an individual. The facade of generality in economic theory might be misleading. We have to be careful and aware that when we take an economic agent to be a group of individuals, the reasonable assumptions we might impose on it are distinct from those we might want to impose on a single individual. For example, although it is quite natural to talk about the will of a person, it is not clear what is meant by the will of a group when the members of the group differ in their preferences.

An economic agent is described in our models as a unit that responds to a scenario called a *choice problem*, where the agent must make a choice from a set of available alternatives. The economic agent appears in the microeconomic model with a specified deliberation process he uses to make a decision. In most of current economic theory, the deliberation process is what is called *rational* choice. The agent decides what action to take through a three-step process:

1. He asks himself, what is desirable?
2. He asks himself, what is feasible?
3. He chooses the most desirable from among the feasible alternatives.

Note the order of the stages. In particular, the stage in which desires are shaped precedes the stage in which feasible alternatives are recognized, and therefore the rational economic agent's desires are independent of the set of alternatives. Note that rationality in economics does not contain judgments about desires. A rational agent can have preferences that the entire world views as being against the agent's interest.

Furthermore, economists are fully aware that almost all people, almost all the time, do not practice this kind of deliberation. Nevertheless, until recently the practice of most economists was to make further assumptions that emphasize the materialist desires of the economic agent and minimize the role of the psychological motives. This practice has been somewhat changed in the past few years with the development of the "Economics and Psychology" approach. Still, we find the investigation of economic agents who follow the rational process to be important, because we often refer to rational decision making in life as an ideal process. It is meaningful to talk about the concept of "being good" even in a society where all people are evil; similarly, it is meaningful to talk about the concept of a "rational man" and about the interactions between rational economic agents even if all people systematically behave in a nonrational manner.

Bibliographic Notes

For an extended discussion of my views about economic theory, see Rubinstein (2006).

Lecture Notes in
Microeconomic Theory

Preferences

Preferences

Our economic agent will soon be advancing to the stage of economic models. Which of his characteristics will we be specifying in order to get him ready? We might have thought name, age and gender, personal history, cognitive abilities and knowledge, and his mental state. However, in most of economic theory, we specify an economic agent only by his attitude toward the elements in some relevant set, and usually we assume that his attitude is expressed in the form of *preferences*.

We begin the course with a modeling "exercise": we seek to develop a "proper" formalization of the concept of preferences. Although we are on our way to constructing a model of rational choice, we will think about the concept of preferences here independently of choice. This is quite natural. We often use the concept of preferences not in the context of choice. For example, we talk about an individual's tastes over the paintings of the masters even if he never makes a decision based on those preferences. We refer to the preferences of an agent were he to arrive tomorrow on Mars or travel back in time and become King David even if he does not believe in the supernatural.

Imagine that you want to fully describe the preferences of an agent toward the elements in a given set X. For example, imagine that you want to describe your own attitude toward the universities you apply to before finding out to which of them you have been admitted. What must the description include? What conditions must the description fulfill?

We take the approach that a description of preferences should fully specify the attitude of the agent toward each pair of elements in X. For each pair of alternatives, it should provide an answer to the question of how the agent compares the two alternatives. We present two versions of this question. For each version, we formulate the consistency requirements necessary to make the responses "preferences" and examine the connection between the two formalizations.

The Questionnaire Q

Let us think about the preferences on a set X as *answers* to a long questionnaire Q that consists of all quiz questions of the type:

$Q(x,y)$ (for all distinct x and y in X):
How do you compare x and y? Tick one and only one of the following three options:

☐ I prefer x to y (this answer is denoted as $x \succ y$).
☐ I prefer y to x (this answer is denoted by $y \succ x$).
☐ I am indifferent (this answer is denoted by I).

A "legal" answer to the questionnaire is a response in which exactly one of the boxes is ticked in each question. We do not allow refraining from answering a question or ticking more than one answer. Furthermore, by allowing only the above three options we exclude responses that demonstrate:

a lack of ability to compare, such as

☐ They are incomparable.
☐ I don't know what x is.
☐ I have no opinion.
☐ I prefer both x over y and y over x.

a dependence on other factors, such as

☐ It depends on what my parents think.
☐ It depends on the circumstances (sometimes I prefer x, but usually I prefer y).

and, most importantly, intensity of preferences, such as

☐ I somewhat prefer x.
☐ I love x and I hate y.

The constraints that we place on the legal responses of the agents constitute our implicit assumptions. Particularly important are the assumption that the elements in the set X are all comparable and the fact that we ignore the intensity of preferences.

A legal answer to the questionnaire can be formulated as a function f, which assigns to any pair (x, y) of distinct elements in X exactly one of the three "values", $x \succ y$ or $y \succ x$ or I, with the interpretation that $f(x, y)$ is the answer to the question $Q(x, y)$. (Alternatively, we can use the notation of the soccer betting industry and say that $f(x, y)$ must be 1, 2, or × with the interpretation that $f(x,y) = 1$ means that x is preferred to y, $f(x,y) = 2$ means that y is preferred to x, and $f(x,y) = \times$ means indifference.)

Not all legal answers to the questionnaire Q qualify as *preferences over the set* X. We will adopt two "consistency" restrictions:

First, the answer to $Q(x,y)$ must be identical to the answer to $Q(y,x)$. In other words, we want to exclude the common "framing effect" by which people who are asked to compare two alternatives tend to prefer the first one.

Second, we require that the answers to $Q(x,y)$ and $Q(y,z)$ are consistent with the answer to $Q(x,z)$ in the following sense. If the answers to the two questions $Q(x,y)$ and $Q(y,z)$ are "x is preferred to y" and "y is preferred to z", then the answer to $Q(x,z)$ must be "x is preferred to z", and if the answers to the two questions $Q(x,y)$ and $Q(y,z)$ are "indifference", then so is the answer to $Q(x,z)$.

To summarize, here is my favorite formalization of the notion of preferences:

Definition 1

Preferences on a set X are a function f that assigns to any pair (x,y) of distinct elements in X exactly one of the three "values" $x \succ y$, $y \succ x$, or I so that for any three different elements x, y, and z in X, the following two properties hold:

- *No order effect*: $f(x,y) = f(y,x)$.
- *Transitivity*:
  if $f(x,y) = x \succ y$ and $f(y,z) = y \succ z$, then $f(x,z) = x \succ z$ and
  if $f(x,y) = I$ and $f(y,z) = I$, then $f(x,z) = I$.

Note again that I, $x \succ y$, and $y \succ x$ are merely symbols representing verbal answers. Needless to say, the choice of symbols is not an arbitrary one. (Why do I use the notation I and not $x \sim y$?)

A Discussion of Transitivity

Transitivity is an appealing property of preferences. How would you react if somebody told you he prefers x to y, y to z, and z to x? You would probably feel that his answers are "confused". Furthermore, it seems that, when confronted with an intransitivity in their responses, people are embarrassed and want to change their answers.

On some occasions before giving this lecture, I asked students to fill out a questionnaire similar to Q regarding a set X that contains nine alternatives, each specifying the following four characteristics of a travel package: location (Paris or Rome), price, quality of the food, and quality of the lodgings. The questionnaire included only thirty-six questions since for each pair of alternatives x and y, only one of the questions, $Q(x, y)$ or $Q(y, x)$, was randomly selected to appear in the questionnaire (thus the dependence on order of an individual's response was not checked within the experimental framework). Out of 458 students who responded to the questionnaire, only 57 (12%) had no intransitivities in their answers, and the median number of triples in which intransitivity existed was 7. Many of the violations of transitivity involved two alternatives that were actually the same but differed in the order in which the characteristics appeared in the description: "A weekend in Paris at a 4-star hotel with food quality Zagat 17 for $574", and "A weekend in Paris for $574 with food quality Zagat 17 at a 4-star hotel". All students expressed indifference between the two alternatives, but in a comparison of these two alternatives to a third alternative—"A weekend in Rome at a 5-star hotel with food quality Zagat 18 for $612"— a quarter of the students gave responses that violated transitivity.

In spite of the appeal of the transitivity requirement, note that when we assume that the attitude of an individual toward pairs of alternatives is transitive, we are excluding individuals who base their judgments on procedures that cause systematic violations of transitivity. The following are two such examples.

1. *Aggregation of considerations as a source of intransitivity.* In some cases, an individual's attitude is derived from the aggregation of more basic considerations. Consider, for example, a case where $X = \{a, b, c\}$ and the individual has three primitive considerations in mind. The individual finds an alternative x better than an alternative y if a majority of considerations supports x. This aggregation process can yield intransitivities. For example, if the three considerations rank the alternatives as $a \succ_1 b \succ_1 c$, $b \succ_2 c \succ_2 a$, and $c \succ_3 a \succ_3 b$, then the individual determines a to be preferred over b, b over c, and c over a, thus violating transitivity.

2. *The use of similarities as an obstacle to transitivity.* In some cases, an individual may express indifference in a comparison between two elements that are too "close" to be distinguishable. For example, let $X = \mathbb{R}$ (the set of real numbers). Consider an individual whose

attitude toward the alternatives is "the larger the better"; however, he finds it impossible to determine whether a is greater than b unless the difference is at least 1. He will assign $f(x, y) = x \succ y$ if $x \geq y + 1$ and $f(x, y) = I$ if $|x - y| < 1$. This is not a preference relation because $1.5 \sim 0.8$ and $0.8 \sim 0.3$, but it is not true that $1.5 \sim 0.3$.

Did we require too little? Another potential criticism of our definition is that our assumptions might have been too weak and that we did not impose some reasonable further restrictions on the concept of preferences. That is, there are other similar consistency requirements we may want to impose on a legal response to qualify it as a description of preferences. For example, if $f(x, y) = x \succ y$ and $f(y, z) = I$, we would naturally expect that $f(x, z) = x \succ z$. However, this additional consistency condition was not included in the above definition because it follows from the other conditions: if $f(x, z) = I$, then by the assumption that $f(y, z) = I$ and by the no order effect, $f(z, y) = I$, and thus by transitivity $f(x, y) = I$ (a contradiction). Alternatively, if $f(x, z) = z \succ x$, then by the no order effect $f(z, x) = z \succ x$, and by $f(x, y) = x \succ y$ and transitivity $f(z, y) = z \succ y$ (a contradiction).

Similarly, note that for any preferences f, we have that if $f(x, y) = I$ and $f(y, z) = y \succ z$, then $f(x, z) = x \succ z$.

The Questionnaire R

A second way to think about preferences is through an imaginary questionnaire R consisting of all questions of the type:

R(x,y) (for all $x, y \in X$, not necessarily distinct):
Is x at least as preferred as y? Tick one and only one of the following two options:

☐ Yes
☐ No

By a "legal" response we mean that the respondent ticks exactly one of the boxes in each question. To qualify as preferences, a legal response must also satisfy two conditions:

1. The answer to at least one of the questions $R(x, y)$ and $R(y, x)$ must be Yes. (In particular, the "silly" question $R(x, x)$ that appears in the questionnaire must get a Yes response.)

2. For every $x, y, z \in X$, if the answers to the questions $R(x, y)$ and $R(y, z)$ are Yes, then so is the answer to the question $R(x, z)$.

We identify a response to this questionnaire with the binary relation $\succsim$ on the set X defined by $x \succsim y$ if the answer to the question $R(x, y)$ is Yes.

(*Reminder*: An *n-ary relation* on X is a subset of X^n. Examples: "Being a parent of" is a binary relation on the set of human beings; "being a hat" is an unary relation on the set of objects; "$x + y = z$" is a 3-ary relation on the set of numbers; "x is better than y more than x' is better than y'" is 4-ary relation on a set of alternatives, etc. An *n-ary relation* on X can be thought of as a response to a questionnaire regarding all n-tuples of elements of X where each question can get only a Yes/No answer.)

This brings us to the traditional definition of preferences.

Definition 2

Preferences on a set X is a binary relation $\succsim$ on X satisfying:

- *Completeness*: For any $x, y \in X$, $x \succsim y$, or $y \succsim x$.
- *Transitivity*: For any $x, y, z \in X$, if $x \succsim y$ and $y \succsim z$, then $x \succsim z$.

The Equivalence of the Two Definitions

We will now discuss the sense in which the two definitions of preferences on the set X are equivalent. But first it is useful to recall the following definitions:

Definitions

The function $f : X \to Y$ is a *one-to-one function* (or *injection*) if $f(x) = f(y)$ implies that $x = y$.

The function $f : X \to Y$ is an *onto function* (or *surjection*) if for every $y \in Y$ there is an $x \in X$ such that $f(x) = y$.

The function $f : X \to Y$ is a *one-to-one and onto function* (or *bijection*, or *one-to-one correspondence*) if for every $y \in Y$ there is a unique $x \in X$ such that $f(x) = y$.

When we think about the equivalence of two definitions in economics, we are thinking about much more than the existence of a one-to-one correspondence: the correspondence also has to *preserve the interpretation*. Note the similarity to the notion of an isomorphism in mathematics

Table 1.1

A response to:	A response to:	
$Q(x,y)$ and $Q(y,x)$	$R(x,y)$ and $R(y,x)$	
$x \succ y$	Yes	No
I	Yes	Yes
$y \succ x$	No	Yes

where a correspondence has to preserve "structure". For example, an isomorphism between two topological spaces X and Y is a one-to-one function from X onto Y that is required to preserve the open sets. In economics, the analogue to "structure" is the less formal notion of interpretation.

We will now construct a one-to-one and onto function, named *Translation*, between answers to Q that qualify as preferences by the first definition and answers to R that qualify as preferences by the second definition, such that the correspondence preserves the meaning of the responses to the two questionnaires.

To illustrate, imagine that you have two books. Each page in the first book is a response to the questionnaire Q that qualifies as preferences by the first definition. Each page in the second book is a response to the questionnaire R that qualifies as preferences by the second definition. The correspondence matches each page in the first book with a unique page in the second book, so that a reasonable person will recognize that the different responses to the two questionnaires reflect the same mental attitudes toward the alternatives.

Since we assume that the answers to all questions of the type $R(x,x)$ are Yes, the classification of a response to R as preferences requires only the specification of the answers to questions $R(x,y)$, where $x \neq y$. Table 1.1 presents the translation of responses.

This translation preserves the interpretation we have given to the responses. That is, if the response to the questionnaire Q exhibits that "I prefer x to y", then the translation to a response to the questionnaire R contains the statement "I find x to be at least as good as y, but I don't find y to be at least as good as x" and thus exhibits the same meaning. Similarly, the translation of a response to Q that exhibits "I am indifferent between x and y" is translated into a response to R that contains the statement "I find x to be at least as good as y, and I find y to be at least as good as x" and thus exhibits the same meaning.

The following observations provide the proof that *Translation* is indeed a one-to-one correspondence between the set of preferences, as given by definition 1, and the set of preferences as given by definition 2.

By the assumption on Q of a no order effect, for any two alternatives x and y, one and only one of the following three answers could have been received for both $Q(x, y)$ and $Q(y, x)$: $x \succ y$, I, and $y \succ x$. Thus, the responses to $R(x, y)$ and $R(y, x)$ are well defined.

Next we verify that the response to R that we have constructed with the table is indeed a preference relation (by the second definition).

Completeness: In each of the three rows, the answers to at least one of the questions $R(x, y)$ and $R(y, x)$ is affirmative.

Transitivity: Assume that the answers to $R(x, y)$ and $R(y, z)$ are affirmative. This implies that the answer to $Q(x, y)$ is either $x \succ y$ or I, and the answer to $Q(y, z)$ is either $y \succ z$ or I. Transitivity of Q implies that the answer to $Q(x, z)$ must be $x \succ z$ or I, and therefore the answer to $R(x, z)$ must be affirmative.

To see that *Translation* is indeed a one-to-one function, note that for any two different responses to the questionnaire Q there must be a question $Q(x, y)$ for which the responses differ; therefore, the corresponding responses to either $R(x, y)$ or $R(y, x)$ must differ.

It remains to be shown that the range of the *Translation* function includes all possible preferences as defined by the second definition. Let $\succsim$ be preferences in the traditional sense (a response to R). We have to specify a function f, a response to Q, which is converted by *Translation* to $\succsim$. Read from right to left, the table provides us with such a function f.

By the completeness of $\succsim$, for any two elements x and y, one of the entries in the right-hand column is applicable (the fourth option, that the two answers to $R(x, y)$ and $R(y, x)$ are No, is excluded), and thus the response to Q is well defined and by definition satisfies no order effect.

We still have to check that f satisfies the transitivity condition. If $f(x, y) = x \succ y$ and $f(y, z) = y \succ z$, then $x \succsim y$ and not $y \succsim x$ and $y \succsim z$ and not $z \succsim y$. By transitivity of $\succsim$, $x \succsim z$. In addition, not $z \succsim x$ since if $z \succsim x$, then the transitivity of $\succsim$ would imply $z \succsim y$. If $f(x, y) = I$ and $f(y, z) = I$, then $x \succsim y$, $y \succsim x$, $y \succsim z$, and $z \succsim y$. By transitivity of $\succsim$, both $x \succsim z$ and $z \succsim x$, and thus $f(x, z) = I$.

Summary

I could have replaced the entire lecture with the following two sentences: "Preferences on X are a binary relation $\succsim$ on a set X satisfying completeness and transitivity. Notate $x \succ y$ when both $x \succsim y$ and not $y \succsim x$, and $x \sim y$ when $x \succsim y$ and $y \succsim x$". However, the role of this chapter was not just to introduce a formal definition of preferences but also to conduct a modeling exercise and to make two methodological points:

1. When we introduce two formalizations of the same verbal concept, we have to make sure that they indeed carry the same meaning.
2. When we construct a formal concept, we make assumptions beyond those explicitly mentioned. Being aware of the implicit assumptions is important for understanding the concept and is useful in coming up with ideas for alternative formalizations.

Bibliographic Notes

Recommended readings.   Kreps 1990, 17–24; Mas-Colell et al. 1995, chapter 1, A–B.

Fishburn (1970) contains a comprehensive treatment of preference relations.

Problem Set 1

Problem 1. (*Easy*)
Let $\succsim$ be a preference relation on a set X. Define $I(x)$ to be the set of all $y \in X$ for which $y \sim x$.

Show that the set (of sets!) $\{I(x) | x \in X\}$ is a partition of X, that is,

- For all x and y, either $I(x) = I(y)$ or $I(x) \cap I(y) = \emptyset$.
- For every $x \in X$, there is $y \in X$ such that $x \in I(y)$.

Problem 2. (*Standard*)
Kreps (1990) introduces another formal definition for preferences. His primitive is a binary relation P interpreted as "strictly preferred". He requires P to satisfy:

- *Asymmetry*: For no x and y do we have both xPy and yPx.
- *Negative Transitivity*: For all x, y, and $z \in X$, if xPy, then for any z either xPz or zPy (or both).

Explain the sense in which Kreps's formalization is equivalent to the traditional definition.

Problem 3. (*Difficult. Based on Kannai and Peleg (1984).*)
Let Z be a finite set and let X be the set of all nonempty subsets of Z. Let $\succsim$ be a preference relation on X (not Z).

Consider the following two properties of preference relations on X:

1. If $A \succsim B$ and C is a set disjoint to both A and B, then $A \cup C \succsim B \cup C$, and
   if $A \succ B$ and C is a set disjoint to both A and B, then $A \cup C \succ B \cup C$.
2. If $x \in Z$ and $\{x\} \succ \{y\}$ for all $y \in A$, then $A \cup \{x\} \succ A$, and
   if $x \in Z$ and $\{y\} \succ \{x\}$ for all $y \in A$, then $A \succ A \cup \{x\}$.

a. Discuss the plausibility of the properties in the context of interpreting $\succsim$ as the attitude of the individual toward sets from which he will have to make a choice at a "second stage".

b. Provide an example of a preference relation that (i) Satisfies the two properties. (ii) Satisfies the first but not the second property. (iii) Satisfies the second but not the first property.

c. Show that if there are x, y, and $z \in Z$ such that $\{x\} \succ \{y\} \succ \{z\}$, then there is no preference relation satisfying both properties.

Problem 4. (*Moderately difficult*)

Let $\succ$ be an asymmetric binary relation on a finite set X that does not have cycles. Show (by induction on the size of X) that $\succ$ can be extended to a complete ordering (i.e., a complete, asymmetric, and transitive binary relation).

Problem 5. (*Fun*)

Listen to the illusion called the Shepard Scale. (You can find it on the Internet. Currently, it is available at http://www.youtube.com/watch?v= ev9hrqkhWsM.)

Can you think of any economic analogies?

Utility

The Concept of Utility Representation

Think of examples of preferences. In the case of a small number of alternatives, we often describe a preference relation as a list arranged from best to worst. In some cases, the alternatives are grouped into a small number of categories, and we describe the preferences on X by specifying the preferences on the set of categories. But, in my experience, most of the examples that come to mind are similar to: "I prefer the taller basketball player", "I prefer the more expensive present", "I prefer a teacher who gives higher grades", "I prefer the person who weighs less". Common to all these examples is that they can naturally be specified by a statement of the form "$x \succsim y$ if $V(x) \geq V(y)$" (or $V(x) \leq V(y)$), where $V : X \to \mathbb{R}$ is a function that attaches a real number to each element in the set of alternatives X. For example, the preferences stated by "I prefer the taller basketball player" can be expressed formally by: X is the set of all conceivable basketball players, and $V(x)$ is the height of player x.

Note that the statement $x \succsim y$ if $V(x) \geq V(y)$ always defines a preference relation because the relation $\geq$ on $\mathbb{R}$ satisfies completeness and transitivity.

Even when the description of a preference relation does not involve a numerical evaluation, we are interested in an equivalent numerical representation. We say that *the function $U : X \to \mathbb{R}$ represents the preference $\succsim$ if for all x and $y \in X$, $x \succsim y$ if and only if $U(x) \geq U(y)$. If the function U represents the preference relation $\succsim$, we refer to it as a *utility function*, and we say that $\succsim$ has a *utility representation*.

It is possible to avoid the notion of a utility representation and to "do economics" with the notion of preferences. Nevertheless, we usually use utility functions rather than preferences as a means of describing an economic agent's attitude toward alternatives, probably because we find it more convenient to talk about the maximization of a numerical function than of a preference relation.

Note that when defining a preference relation using a utility function, the function has an intuitive meaning that carries with it additional information. In contrast, when the utility function is formed in order to represent an existing preference relation, the utility function has no meaning other than that of representing a preference relation. Absolute numbers are meaningless in the latter case; only relative order has meaning. Indeed, if a preference relation has a utility representation, then it has an infinite number of such representations, as the following simple claim shows:

Claim:

If U represents $\succsim$, then for any strictly increasing function $f : \mathbb{R} \to \mathbb{R}$, the function $V(x) = f(U(x))$ represents $\succsim$ as well.

Proof:

$a \succsim b$
iff $U(a) \geq U(b)$ (since U represents $\succsim$)
iff $f(U(a)) \geq f(U(b))$ (since f is strictly increasing)
iff $V(a) \geq V(b)$.

Existence of a Utility Representation

If any preference relation could be represented by a utility function, then it would "grant a license" to use utility functions rather than preference relations with no loss of generality. Utility theory investigates the possibility of using a numerical function to represent a preference relation and the possibility of numerical representations carrying additional meanings (e.g., a is preferred to b more than c is preferred to d).

We will now examine the basic question of "utility theory": Under what assumptions do utility representations exist?

Our first observation is quite trivial. When the set X is finite, there is always a utility representation. The detailed proof is presented here mainly to get into the habit of analytical precision. We start with a lemma regarding the existence of minimal elements (an element $a \in X$ is *minimal* if $a \precsim x$ for any $x \in X$).

Lemma:

In any finite set $A \subseteq X$, there is a minimal element (similarly, there is also a maximal element).

Proof:

By induction on the size of A. If A is a singleton, then by completeness its only element is minimal. For the inductive step, let A be of cardinality $n+1$ and let $x \in A$. The set $A-\{x\}$ is of cardinality n and by the inductive assumption has a minimal element denoted by y. If $x \succsim y$, then y is minimal in A. If $y \succsim x$, then by transitivity $z \succsim x$ for all $z \in A-\{x\}$, and thus x is minimal.

Claim:

If $\succsim$ is a preference relation on a finite set X, then $\succsim$ has a utility representation with values being natural numbers.

Proof:

We will construct a sequence of sets inductively. Let X_1 be the subset of elements that are minimal in X. By the above lemma, X_1 is not empty. Assume we have constructed the sets $X_1, \ldots, X_k$. If $X = X_1 \cup X_2 \cup \ldots \cup X_k$, we are done. If not, define X_{k+1} to be the set of minimal elements in $X - X_1 - X_2 - \cdots - X_k$. By the lemma $X_{k+1} \neq \emptyset$. Because X is finite, we must be done after at most $|X|$ steps. Define $U(x) = k$ if $x \in X_k$. Thus, $U(x)$ is the step number at which x is "eliminated". To verify that U represents $\succsim$, let $a \succ b$. Then $a \notin X_1 \cup X_2 \cup \cdots X_{U(b)}$ and thus $U(a) > U(b)$. If $a \sim b$, then clearly $U(a) = U(b)$.

Without any further assumptions on the preferences, the existence of a utility representation is guaranteed when the set X is countable (recall that X is countable and infinite if there is a one-to-one function from the natural numbers onto X, namely, it is possible to specify an enumeration of all its members $\{x_n\}_{n=1,2,\ldots}$).

Claim:

If X is countable, then any preference relation on X has a utility representation with a range $(-1, 1)$.

Proof:

Let $\{x_n\}$ be an enumeration of all elements in X. We will construct the utility function inductively. Set $U(x_1) = 0$. Assume that you have completed the definition of the values $U(x_1), \ldots, U(x_{n-1})$ so that $x_k \succsim x_l$ iff $U(x_k) \geq U(x_l)$. If x_n is indifferent to x_k for some $k < n$, then assign

$U(x_n) = U(x_k)$. If not, by transitivity, all numbers in the nonempty set $\{U(x_k)|\ x_k \prec x_n\} \cup \{-1\}$ are below all numbers in the nonempty set $\{U(x_k)|\ x_n \prec x_k\} \cup \{1\}$. Choose $U(x_n)$ to be between the two sets. This guarantees that for any $k < n$ we have $x_n \succsim x_k$ iff $U(x_n) \geq U(x_k)$. Thus, the function we defined on $\{x_1, \ldots, x_n\}$ represents the preferences on those elements.

To complete the proof that U represents $\succsim$, take any two elements, x and $y \in X$. For some k and l we have $x = x_k$ and $y = x_l$. The above applied to $n = \max\{k, l\}$ yields $x_k \succsim x_l$ iff $U(x_k) \geq U(x_l)$.

Lexicographic Preferences

Lexicographic preferences are the outcome of applying the following procedure for determining the ranking of any two elements in a set X. The individual has in mind a sequence of criteria that could be used to compare pairs of elements in X. The criteria are applied in a fixed order until a criterion is reached that succeeds in distinguishing between the two elements, in that it determines the preferred alternative. Formally, let $(\succsim_k)_{k=1,\ldots,K}$ be a K-tuple of preferences over the set X. The lexicographic preferences induced by those preferences are defined by $x \succsim_L y$ if (1) there is k^* such that for all $k < k^*$ we have $x \sim_k y$ and $x \succ_{k*} y$ or (2) $x \sim_k y$ for all k. Verify that $\succsim_L$ is a preference relation.

Example:
Let X be the unit square, that is, $X = [0,1] \times [0,1]$. Let $x \succsim_k y$ if $x_k \geq y_k$. The lexicographic preferences $\succsim_L$ induced from $\succsim_1$ and $\succsim_2$ are: $(a_1, a_2) \succsim_L (b_1, b_2)$ if $a_1 > b_1$ or both $a_1 = b_1$ and $a_2 \geq b_2$. (Thus, in this example, the left component is the primary criterion, whereas the right component is the secondary criterion.)

We will now show that the preferences $\succsim_L$ do *not* have a utility representation. The lack of a utility representation excludes lexicographic preferences from the scope of standard economic models, although they are derived from a simple and commonly used procedure.

Claim:
The lexicographic preference relation $\succsim_L$ on $[0,1] \times [0,1]$, induced from the relations $x \succsim_k y$ if $x_k \geq y_k$ $(k = 1, 2)$, does not have a utility representation.

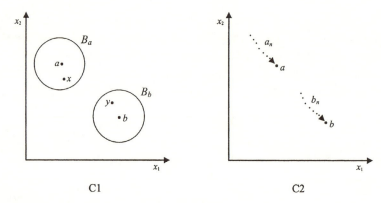

Figure 2.1
Two definitions of continuity of preferences.

Proof:

Assume by contradiction that the function $u : X \to \mathbb{R}$ represents $\succsim_L$. For any $a \in [0,1]$, $(a,1) \succ_L (a,0)$, we thus have $u(a,1) > u(a,0)$. Let $q(a)$ be a rational number in the nonempty interval $I_a = (u(a,0), u(a,1))$. The function q is a function from $[0,1]$ into the set of rational numbers. It is a one-to-one function since if $b > a$, then $(b,0) \succ_L (a,1)$ and therefore $u(b,0) > u(a,1)$. It follows that the intervals I_a and I_b are disjoint and thus $q(a) \neq q(b)$. But the cardinality of the rational numbers is lower than that of the continuum, a contradiction.

Continuity of Preferences

In economics we often take the set X to be an infinite subset of a Euclidean space. The following is a condition that will guarantee the existence of a utility representation in such a case. The basic intuition, captured by the notion of a continuous preference relation, is that if a is preferred to b, then "small" deviations from a or from b will not reverse the ordering.

In what follows we will refer to a *ball* around a in X with radius $r > 0$, denoted as $B(a, r)$, as the set of all points in X that are distanced less than r from a.

Definition C1:

A preference relation $\succsim$ on X is *continuous* if whenever $a \succ b$ (namely, it is not true that $b \succsim a$), there are balls (neighborhoods in the relevant topology) B_a and B_b around a and b, respectively, such that for all $x \in B_a$ and $y \in B_b$, $x \succ y$. (See fig. 2.1.)

Definition C2:

A preference relation $\succsim$ on X is *continuous* if the graph of $\succsim$ (i.e., the set $\{(x,y)|x \succsim y\} \subseteq X \times X)$ is a closed set (with the product topology); that is, if $\{(a_n, b_n)\}$ is a sequence of pairs of elements in X satisfying $a_n \succsim b_n$ for all n and $a_n \to a$ and $b_n \to b$, then $a \succsim b$. (See fig. 2.1.)

Claim:

The preference relation $\succsim$ on X satisfies C1 if and only if it satisfies C2.

Proof:

Assume that $\succsim$ on X is continuous according to C1. Let $\{(a_n, b_n)\}$ be a sequence of pairs satisfying $a_n \succsim b_n$ for all n and $a_n \to a$ and $b_n \to b$. If it is not true that $a \succsim b$ (i.e., $b \succ a$), then there exist two balls B_a and B_b around a and b, respectively, such that for all $y \in B_b$ and $x \in B_a$, $y \succ x$. There is an N large enough such that for all $n > N$, both $b_n \in B_b$ and $a_n \in B_a$. Therefore, for all $n > N$, we have $b_n \succ a_n$, which is a contradiction.

Assume that $\succsim$ is continuous according to C2. Let $a \succ b$. Recall that $B(x, r)$ is the set of all elements in X distanced less than r from x. Assume by contradiction that for all n there exist $a_n \in B(a, 1/n)$ and $b_n \in B(b, 1/n)$ such that $b_n \succsim a_n$. The sequence (b_n, a_n) converges to (b, a); by the second definition, (b, a) is within the graph of $\succsim$, that is, $b \succsim a$, which is a contradiction.

Remarks

1. If $\succsim$ on X is represented by a *continuous* function U, then $\succsim$ is continuous. To see this, note that if $a \succ b$, then $U(a) > U(b)$. Let $\varepsilon = (U(a) - U(b))/2$. By the continuity of U, there is a $\delta > 0$ such that for all x distanced less than δ from a, $U(x) > U(a) - \varepsilon$, and for all y distanced less than δ from b, $U(y) < U(b) + \varepsilon$. Thus, for x and y within the balls of radius δ around a and b, respectively, $x \succ y$.

2. The lexicographic preferences that were used in the counterexample to the existence of a utility representation are not continuous. This is because $(1, 1) \succ (1, 0)$, but in any ball around $(1, 1)$ there are points inferior to $(1, 0)$.

3. Note that the second definition of continuity can be applied to any binary relation over a topological space, not just to a preference relation. For example, the relation $=$ on the real numbers $(\mathbb{R}^1)$ is continuous, whereas the relation $\neq$ is not.

Debreu's Theorem

Debreu's theorem, which states that continuous preferences have a *continuous* utility representation, is one of the classic results in economic theory. For a complete proof of Debreu's theorem, see Debreu (1954, 1960). Here we prove only that continuity guarantees the existence of a utility representation.

Lemma:

If $\succsim$ is a continuous preference relation on a convex set $X \subseteq \mathbb{R}^n$, and if $x \succ y$, then there exists z in X such that $x \succ z \succ y$.

Proof:

Assume not. Let I be the interval that connects x and y. By the convexity of X, $I \subseteq X$. Construct inductively two sequences of points in I, $\{x_t\}$ and $\{y_t\}$, in the following way. First define $x_0 = x$ and $y_0 = y$. Assume that the two points, x_t and y_t are defined, belong to I, and satisfy $x_t \succsim x$ and $y \succsim y_t$. Consider the middle point between x_t and y_t and denote it by m. According to the assumption, either $m \succsim x$ or $y \succsim m$. In the former case define $x_{t+1} = m$ and $y_{t+1} = y_t$, and in the latter case define $x_{t+1} = x_t$ and $y_{t+1} = m$. The sequences $\{x_t\}$ and $\{y_t\}$ are converging, and they must converge to the same point z because the distance between x_t and y_t converges to zero. By the continuity of $\succsim$, we have $z \succsim x$ and $y \succsim z$ and thus, by transitivity, $y \succsim x$, which contradicts the assumption that $x \succ y$.

Comment on the Proof

Another proof could be given for the more general case, in which the assumption that the set X is convex is replaced by the weaker assumption that it is a connected subset of $\mathbb{R}^n$. (Remember that a connected set cannot be covered by two nonempty disjoint open sets.) If there is no z such that $x \succ z \succ y$, then X is the union of two disjoint sets $\{a | a \succ y\}$ and $\{a | x \succ a\}$, which are open by the continuity of the preference relation, which contradicts the connectedness of X.

We say that the set Y is dense in X if every open set $B \subset X$ contains an element in Y. Any set $X \subseteq \mathbb{R}^m$ has a countable dense subset. To see this, note that the standard topology in $\mathbb{R}^m$ has a countable base. That is, any open set is the union of subsets of the countable collection of open sets: $\{B(a, 1/n)|$ all the components of $a \in \mathbb{R}^m$ are rational numbers; n is a natural number$\}$. For every set $B(q, 1/n)$ that intersects X, pick a point $y_{q,n} \in X \cap B(q, 1/n)$. Let Y be the set containing all the points $\{y_{q,n}\}$. This is a countable dense set in X.

Proposition:

Assume that X is a convex subset of $\mathbb{R}^n$. If $\succsim$ is a continuous preference relation on X, then $\succsim$ has a utility representation. (Actually, there is a utility representation that is continuous, but we will not prove this part.)

Proof:

Denote by Y a countable dense set in X. By a previous claim we know that there exists a function $v : Y \to (-1, 1)$, which is a utility representation of the preference relation $\succsim$ restricted to Y. For every $x \in X$, define $U(x) = \sup\{v(z) | z \in Y \text{ and } x \succ z\}$. Define $U(x) = -1$ if there is no $z \in Y$ such that $x \succ z$, which means that x is the minimal element in X. (Note that it could be that $U(z) < v(z)$ for some $z \in Y$.)

If $x \sim y$, then $x \succ z$ iff $y \succ z$. Thus, the sets on which the supremum is taken are the same and $U(x) = U(y)$.

If $x \succ y$, then by the lemma there exists z in X such that $x \succ z \succ y$. By the continuity of the preferences $\succsim$, there is a ball around z such that all the elements in that ball are inferior to x and superior to y. Because Y is dense, there exists $z_1 \in Y$ such that $x \succ z_1 \succ y$. Similarly, there exists $z_2 \in Y$ such that $z_1 \succ z_2 \succ y$. Finally,
$U(x) \geq v(z_1)$ (by the definition of U and $x \succ z_1$),
$v(z_1) > v(z_2)$ (since v represents $\succsim$ on Y and $z_1 \succ z_2$), and
$v(z_2) \geq U(y)$ (by the definition of U and $z_2 \succ y$).

Bibliographic Notes

Recommended readings.   Kreps 1990, 30–32; Mas-Colell et al. 1995, chapter 3, C.

Fishburn (1970) covers the material in this lecture very well. The example of lexicographic preferences originated in Debreu (1959) (see also Debreu (1960), in particular chapter 2, which is available online at http://cowles.econ.yale.edu/P/cp/p00b/p0097.pdf.)

Problem Set 2

Problem 1. (*Easy*)
The purpose of this problem is to make sure that you fully understand the basic concepts of utility representation and continuous preferences.

  a. Is the statement "if both U and V represent $\succsim$, then there is a *strictly monotonic* function $f : \mathbb{R} \to \mathbb{R}$ such that $V(x) = f(U(x))$" correct?
  b. Can a continuous preference relation be represented by a discontinuous utility function?
  c. Show that in the case of $X = \mathbb{R}$, the preference relation that is represented by the discontinuous utility function $u(x) = [x]$ (the largest integer n such that $x \geq n$) is not a continuous relation.
  d. Show that the two definitions of a continuous preference relation (C1 and C2) are equivalent to

> **Definition C3:** For any $x \in X$, the upper and lower contours $\{y|\ y \succsim x\}$ and $\{y|\ x \succsim y\}$ are closed sets in X,

and to

> **Definition C4:** For any $x \in X$, the sets $\{y|\ y \succ x\}$ and $\{y|\ x \succ y\}$ are open sets in X.

Problem 2. (*Moderately difficult*)
Give an example of preferences over a countable set in which the preferences cannot be represented by a utility function that returns only integers as values.

Problem 3. (*Easy*)
Let $\succsim$ be continuous preferences on a set $X \subseteq \mathbb{R}^n$ that contains the interval connecting the points x and z. Show that if $y \in X$ and $x \succsim y \succsim z$, then there is a point m on the interval connecting x and z such that $y \sim m$.

Problem 4. (*Moderately difficult*)
Consider the sequence of preference relations $(\succsim^n)_{n=1,2,\dots}$, defined on $\mathbb{R}^2_+$ where $\succsim^n$ is represented by the utility function $u_n(x_1, x_2) = x_1^n + x_2^n$. We will say that the sequence $\succsim^n$ converges to the preferences $\succsim^*$ if for every x and y, such that $x \succ^* y$, there is an N such that for every $n > N$ we have $x \succ^n y$. Show that the sequence of preference relations $\succsim^n$ converges to the preferences $\succ^*$, which are represented by the function $max\{x_1, x_2\}$.

Problem 5. (*Moderately difficult*)

The following is a typical example of a utility representation theorem:

Let $X = \mathbb{R}^2_+$. Assume that a preference relation $\succsim$ satisfies the following three properties:

ADD: $(a_1, a_2) \succsim (b_1, b_2)$ implies that $(a_1 + t, a_2 + s) \succsim (b_1 + t, b_2 + s)$ for all t and s.

SMON: If $a_1 \geq b_1$ and $a_2 \geq b_2$, then $(a_1, a_2) \succsim (b_1, b_2)$; in addition, if either $a_1 > b_1$ or $a_2 > b_2$, then $(a_1, a_2) \succ (b_1, b_2)$.

CON: Continuity.

    a. Show that, if $\succsim$ has a linear representation (i.e., $\succsim$ is represented by a utility function $u(x_1, x_2) = \alpha x_1 + \beta x_2$ with $\alpha > 0$ and $\beta > 0$), then $\succsim$ satisfies ADD, SMON, and CON.

    b. Show that for any pair of the three properties there is a preference relation that does not satisfy the third property.

    c. (*This part is difficult*) Show that if $\succsim$ satisfies the three properties, then it has a linear representation.

    d. (*This part is also difficult*) Characterize the preference relations that satisfy ADD, SMON, and an additional property MUL:

        MUL: $(a_1, a_2) \succsim (b_1, b_2)$ implies that $(\lambda a_1, \lambda a_2) \succsim (\lambda b_1, \lambda b_2)$ for any positive λ.

Problem 6. (*Moderately difficult*)

    Let X be a finite set and let $(\succsim, \succ\succ)$ be a pair where $\succsim$ is a preference relation and $\succ\succ$ is a transitive subrelation of $\succ$ (by subrelation, we mean that $x \succ\succ y$ implies $x \succ y$.)

    We can think about the pair as representing the responses to the questionnaire A, where $A(x, y)$ is the following question:

How do you compare x and y? Tick one of the following five options:
  ☐ I very much prefer x over y ($x \succ\succ y$).
  ☐ I prefer x over y ($x \succ y$).
  ☐ I am indifferent (I).
  ☐ I prefer y over x ($y \succ x$).
  ☐ I very much prefer y over x ($y \succ\succ x$).

Assume that the pair satisfies extended transitivity:

If $x \succ\succ y$ and $y \succsim z$, or if $x \succsim y$ and $y \succ\succ z$, then $x \succ\succ z$.

    We say that a pair $(\succsim, \succ\succ)$ is represented by a function u if:

$$u(x) = u(y) \text{ iff } x \sim y,$$
$$u(x) - u(y) > 0 \text{ iff } x \succ y, \text{ and}$$
$$u(x) - u(y) > 1 \text{ iff } x \succ\succ y.$$

Show that every extended preference $(\succsim, \succ\succ)$ is represented by a function u.

Problem 7. (*Moderately difficult*)

Utility is a numerical representation of preferences. One can think about the numerical representation of other abstract concepts. Here, you will try to come up with a possible numerical representation of the concept "approximately the same" (see Luce (1956) and Rubinstein (1988)). For simplicity, let X be the interval $[0, 1]$.

Consider the following six properties of the binary relation S:

(S-1) For any $a \in X$, aSa.

(S-2) For all $a, b \in X$, if aSb, then bSa.

(S-3) Continuity (the graph of the relation S in $X \times X$ is a closed set).

(S-4) Betweenness: If $d \geq c \geq b \geq a$ and dSa, then also cSb.

(S-5) For any $a \in X$, there is an open interval around a such that xSa for every x in the interval.

(S-6) Denote $M(a) = max\{x|xSa\}$ and $m(a) = min\{x|aSx\}$. Then, M and m are (weakly) increasing functions and are strictly increasing whenever they do not have the values 0 or 1.

a. Do these assumptions capture your intuition about the concept "approximately the same"?

b. Show that the relation S_ε, defined by $aS_\varepsilon b$ if $|b - a| \leq \varepsilon$ (for positive ε), satisfies all assumptions.

c. (*Difficult*) Let S be a binary relation that satisfies the above six properties and let ε be a strictly positive number. Show that there is a strictly increasing and continuous function $H : X \to \mathbb{R}$ such that aSb if and only if $|H(a) - H(b)| \leq \varepsilon$.

Problem 8. (*Further reading*)

Read Kahneman (2000) and discuss his distinction between the different types of "psychological utilities".

Choice

Choice Functions

Until now we have avoided any reference to behavior. We have talked about preferences as a summary of the decision maker's mental attitude toward a set of alternatives. But economics is about action, and therefore we now move on to modeling "agent behavior". By a description of agent behavior we will refer not only to his actual choices, made when he confronts a certain problem, but to a full description of his behavior in all scenarios we imagine he might confront in a certain context.

Consider a *grand set* X of possible alternatives. We view a *choice problem* as a nonempty subset of X, and we refer to a choice from $A \subseteq X$ as specifying one of A's members.

Modeling a choice scenario as a set of alternatives implies assumptions of rationality according to which the agent's choice does not depend on the way the alternatives are presented. For example, if the alternatives appear in a list, he ignores the order in which they are presented and the number of times an alternative appears in the list. If there is an alternative with a default status, he ignores that as well. As a rational agent he considers only the set of alternatives available to him.

In some contexts, not all choice problems are relevant. Therefore we allow that the agent's behavior be defined only on a set D of subsets of X. We will refer to a pair (X, D) as a *context*.

Example:

1. Imagine that we are interested in a student's behavior regarding his selection from the set of universities to which he has been admitted. Let $X = \{x_1, \ldots, x_N\}$ be the set of all universities with which the student is familiar. A choice problem A is interpreted as the set of universities to which he has been admitted. If the fact that the student was admitted to some subset of universities does not imply his admission outcome for other universities, then D contains the $2^N - 1$ nonempty subsets of X. But if, for example, the universities are listed according to difficulty in

being admitted (x_1 being the most difficult) and if the fact that the student is admitted to x_k means that he is admitted to all less "prestigious" universities, that is, to all x_l with $l > k$, then D will consist of the N sets $A_1, \ldots, A_N$ where $A_k = \{x_k, \ldots, x_N\}$.

2. Imagine a scenario in which a decision maker is choosing whether to remain with the status quo s or choose an element in some set Y. We formalize such a scenario by defining $X = Y \cup \{s\}$ and identifying the domain of the choice function D as the set of all subsets of X that contain s.

We think about an agent's behavior as a hypothetical response to a questionnaire that contains questions of the following type, one for each $A \in D$:

Q(A): Assume you must choose from a set of alternatives A. Which alternative do you choose?

A permissible response to this questionnaire requires that the agent select a unique element in A for every question Q(A). We implicitly assume that the agent cannot give any other answer such as "I choose either a or b"; "the probability of my choosing $a \in A$ is $p(a)$"; or "I don't know".

Formally, given a context (X, D), a *choice function* C assigns to each set $A \in D$ a unique element of A with the interpretation that $C(A)$ is the chosen element from the set A.

Our understanding is that a decision maker behaving in accordance with the function C will choose $C(A)$ if he has to make a choice from a set A. This does not mean that we can actually observe the choice function. At most we might observe some particular choices made by the decision maker in some instances. Thus, a choice function is a description of hypothetical behavior.

Rational Choice Functions

It is typically assumed in economics that choice is an outcome of "rational deliberation". Namely, the decision maker has in mind a preference relation $\succsim$ on the set X and, given any choice problem A in D, he chooses an element in A that is $\succsim$ optimal. Assuming that it is well defined, we define the *induced choice function* $C_\succsim$ as the function that assigns to every nonempty set $A \in D$ the $\succsim$-best element of A. Note that the preference relation is fixed, that is, it is independent of the choice set being considered.

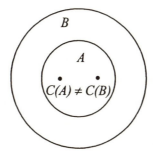

Figure 3.1
Violation of condition α.

Rationalizing

Economists were often criticized for making the assumption that decision makers maximize a preference relation. The most common response to this criticism is that we don't really need this assumption. All we need to assume is that the decision maker's behavior can be described *as if* he were maximizing some preference relation.

Let us state this "economic defense" more precisely. We will say that a choice function C *can be rationalized* if there is a preference relation $\succsim$ on X so that $C = C_{\succsim}$ (i.e., $C(A) = C_{\succsim}(A)$ for any A in the domain of C).

We will now identify a condition under which a choice function can indeed be presented as if derived from some preference relation (i.e., can be rationalized).

Condition α:

We say that C satisfies condition α if for any two problems $A, B \in D$, if $A \subset B$ and $C(B) \in A$, then $C(A) = C(B)$. (See fig. 3.1.)

Note that if $\succsim$ is a preference relation on X, then $C_{\succsim}$ (defined on a set of subsets of X that have a single most preferred element) satisfies condition α.

As an example of a choice procedure that does not satisfy condition α, consider the *second-best procedure*: the decision maker has in mind an ordering $\succsim$ of X (i.e., a complete, asymmetric and transitive binary relation) and for any given choice problem set A chooses the element from A, which is the $\succsim$-maximal from the nonoptimal alternatives. If A contains all the elements in B besides the $\succsim$-maximal, then $C(B) \in A \subset B$ but $C(A) \neq C(B)$.

We will now show that condition α is a sufficient condition for a choice function to be formulated *as if* the decision maker is maximizing some preference relation.

Proposition:
Assume that C is a choice function with a domain containing at least all subsets of X of size 2 or 3. If C satisfies condition α, then there is a preference $\succsim$ on X so that $C = C_{\succsim}$.

Proof:
Define $\succsim$ by $x \succsim y$ if $x = C(\{x, y\})$.

Let us first verify that the relation $\succsim$ is a preference relation.

Completeness: Follows from the fact that $C(\{x, y\})$ is always well defined.

Transitivity: If $x \succsim y$ and $y \succsim z$, then $C(\{x, y\}) = x$ and $C(\{y, z\}) = y$. If $C(\{x, z\}) \neq x$, then $C(\{x, z\}) = z$. By condition α and $C(\{x, z\}) = z$, $C(\{x, y, z\}) \neq x$. By condition α and $C(\{x, y\}) = x$, $C(\{x, y, z\}) \neq y$, and by condition α and $C(\{y, z\}) = y$, $C(\{x, y, z\}) \neq z$. A contradiction to $C(\{x, y, z\}) \in \{x, y, z\}$.

We still have to show that $C(B) = C_{\succsim}(B)$. Assume that $C(B) = x$ and $C_{\succsim}(B) \neq x$. That is, there is $y \in B$ so that $y \succ x$. By definition of $\succsim$, this means $C(\{x, y\}) = y$, contradicting condition α.

Dutch Book Arguments

Some of the justifications for the assumption that choice is determined by "rational deliberation" are normative, that is, they reflect a perception that people should be rational in this sense and, if they are not, they should convert to reasoning of this type. One interesting class of arguments supporting this approach is referred to in the literature as "Dutch book arguments". The claim is that an economic agent who behaves according to a choice function that is not induced from maximization of a preference relation will not survive.

The following is a "sad" story about a monkey in a forest with three trees, a, b, and c. The monkey is about to pick a tree to sleep in. Assume that the monkey can assess only two alternatives at a time and that his choice function is $C(\{a, b\}) = b$, $C(\{b, c\}) = c$, $C(\{a, c\}) = a$. Obviously, his choice function cannot be derived from a preference relation over the set of trees. Assume that whenever he is on tree x it comes to his mind occasionally to jump to one of the other trees; namely, he makes a choice from a set $\{x, y\}$ where y is one of the two other trees. This induces the monkey to perpetually jump from one tree to another – not a particularly desirable mode of behavior in the jungle.

Another argument – which is more appropriate to human beings – is called the "money pump" argument. Assume that a decision maker behaves like the monkey with respect to three alternatives a, b, and c. Assume that, for all x and y, the choice $C(x, y) = y$ is strong enough so that whenever he is about to choose alternative x and somebody gives him the option to also choose y, he is ready to pay one cent for the opportunity to do so. Now, imagine a manipulator who presents the agent with the choice problem $\{a, b, c\}$. Whenever the decision maker is about to make the choice a, the manipulator allows him to revise his choice to b for one cent. Similarly, every time he is about to choose b or c, the manipulator sells him for one cent the opportunity to choose c or a accordingly. The decision maker will cycle through the intentions to choose a, b, and c until his pockets are emptied or until he learns his lesson and changes his behavior.

The above arguments are open to criticism. In particular, the elimination of patterns of behavior that are inconsistent with rationality require an environment in which the economic agent is indeed confronted with the above sequence of choice problems. The arguments are presented here as interesting ideas and not necessarily as convincing arguments for rationality.

What Is an Alternative

Some of the cases where rationality is violated can be attributed to the incorrect specification of the space of alternatives. Consider the following example taken from Luce and Raiffa (1957): a diner in a restaurant chooses *chicken* from the menu *steak tartare, chicken* but chooses *steak tartare* from the menu *steak tartare, chicken, frog legs*. At first glance it seems that he is not rational (since his choice conflicts with condition α). Assume that the motivation for the choice is that the existence of *frog legs* is an indication of the quality of the chef. If the dish *frog legs* is on the menu, the cook must then be a real expert, and the decision maker is happy ordering *steak tartare*, which requires expertise to make. If the menu lacks *frog legs*, the decision maker does not want to take the risk of choosing *steak tartare*.

Rationality is "restored" if we make the distinction between "*steak tartare* served in a restaurant where *frog legs* are also on the menu (and the cook must then be a real chef)" and "*steak tartare* in a restaurant where *frog legs* are not served (and the cook is likely a novice)". Such a distinction makes sense because the *steak tartare* is not the same in the two choice sets.

Note that if we define an alternative to be (a, A), where a is a physical description and A is the choice problem, any choice function C can be rationalized by a preference relation satisfying $(C(A), A) \succsim (a, A)$ for every $a \in A$.

The lesson to be learned from the above discussion is that care must be taken in specifying the term "alternative". An alternative a must have the same meaning for every A which contains a.

Choice Functions as Internal Equilibria

The choice function definition we have been using requires that a single element be assigned to each choice problem. If the decision maker follows the rational man procedure using a preference relation with indifferences, the previously defined induced choice function $C_{\succsim}(A)$ might be undefined because for some choice problems there would be more than one optimal element. This is one of the reasons that in some cases we use the alternative following concept to model behavior.

A *choice correspondence* C is required to assign to every nonempty $A \subseteq X$ a nonempty *subset* of A, that is, $\emptyset \neq C(A) \subseteq A$. According to our interpretation of a choice problem, a decision maker has to select a unique element from every choice set. Thus, $C(A)$ cannot be interpreted as the choice made by the decision maker when he has to make a choice from A. The revised interpretation of $C(A)$ is the *set* of all elements in A that are satisfactory in the sense that if the decision maker is about to make a decision and choose $a \in C(A)$, he has no desire to move away from it. In other words, the induced choice correspondence reflects an "internal equilibrium": if the decision maker facing A considers an alternative outside $C(A)$, he will continue searching for another alternative. If he happens to consider an alternative inside $C(A)$, he will take it.

A related interpretation of $C(A)$ involves viewing it as the set of all elements in A that may be chosen under any of many possible particular circumstances not included in the description of the set A. Formally, let (A, f) be an extended choice set where f is the frame that accompanies the set A (like the default alternative or the order of the alternatives). Let $c(A, f)$ be the choice of the decision maker from the choice set A given the frame f. The (extended) choice function c induces a choice correspondence by $C(A) = \{x | x = c(A, f) \text{ for some } f\}$.

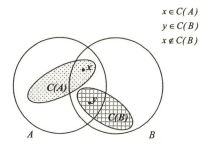

Figure 3.2
Violation of the weak axiom.

Given a preference relation $\succsim$ we define the induced choice function (assuming it is never empty) as $C_{\succsim}(A) = \{x \in A \mid x \succsim y \text{ for all } y \in A\}$.

When $x, y \in A$ and $x \in C(A)$, we say that x is revealed to be at least as good as y. If, in addition, $y \notin C(A)$, we say that x is revealed to be strictly better than y. Condition α is now replaced by condition WA, which requires that if x is revealed to be at least as good as y, then y is not revealed to be strictly better than x.

The Weak Axiom of Revealed Preference (WA):
We say that C satisfies WA if whenever $x, y \in A \cap B$, $x \in C(A)$, and $y \in C(B)$, it is also true that $x \in C(B)$ (fig. 3.2).

The Weak Axiom trivially implies two properties: *Condition α*: If $a \in A \subset B$ and $a \in C(B)$, then $a \in C(A)$. *Condition β*: If $a, b \in A \subset B$, $a \in c(A)$, and $b \in C(B)$, then $a \in C(B)$.

Notice that if $C(A)$ contains all elements that are maximal according to some preference relation, then C satisfies WA. Also, verify that conditions α and WA are equivalent for any choice function with a domain satisfying that if A and B are included in the domain, then so is their intersection. Note also that for the next proposition, we could make do with a weaker version of WA, which makes the same requirement only for any two sets $A \subset B$ where A is a set of two elements.

Proposition:
Assume that C is a choice correspondence with a domain that includes at least all subsets of size 2 or 3. Assume that C satisfies WA. Then, there is a preference $\succsim$ so that $C = C_{\succsim}$.

Proof:

Define $x \succsim y$ if $x \in C(\{x, y\})$. We will now show that the relation is a preference:

Completeness: Follows from $C(\{x, y\}) \neq \emptyset$.

Transitivity: If $x \succsim y$ and $y \succsim z$, then $x \in C(\{x, y\})$ and $y \in C(\{y, z\})$. Therefore, by condition β, if $y \in C(\{x, y, z\})$, then $x \in C(\{x, y, z\})$, and if $z \in C(\{x, y, z\})$, then $y \in C(\{x, y, z\})$. Thus, in any case, $x \in C(\{x, y, z\})$. By condition α, $x \in C(\{x, z\})$ and thus $x \succsim z$.

It remains to be shown that $C(B) = C_{\succsim}(B)$.

Assume that $x \in C(B)$ and $x \notin C_{\succsim}(B)$. That is, there is $y \in B$ so that it is not true that $x \succsim y$ or, in other words, $C(\{x, y\}) = \{y\}$, thus contradicting condition α.

Assume that $x \in C_{\succsim}(B)$ and $x \notin C(B)$. Let $y \in C(B)$. By condition β, $x \notin C(\{x, y\})$ and thus $C(\{x, y\}) = \{y\}$. Therefore $y \succ x$, contradicting $x \in C_{\succsim}(B)$.

The Satisficing Procedure

The fact that we can present any choice function satisfying condition α (or WA) as an outcome of the optimization of some preference relation provides support for the view that the scope of microeconomic models is wider than simply models in which agents carry out explicit optimization. But have we indeed expanded the scope of economic models?

Consider the following "decision scheme", named *satisficing* by Herbert Simon. Let $v : X \to \mathbb{R}$ be a valuation of the elements in X, and let $v^* \in \mathbb{R}$ be a threshold of satisfaction. Let O be an ordering of the alternatives in X. Given a set A, the decision maker arranges the elements of this set in a list $L(A, O)$ according to the ordering O. He then chooses the first element in $L(A, O)$ that has a v-value at least as large as v^*. If there is no such element in A, the decision maker chooses the last element in $L(A, O)$.

Let us show that the choice function induced by this procedure satisfies condition α. Assume that a is chosen from B and is also a member of $A \subset B$. The list $L(A, O)$ is obtained from $L(B, O)$ by eliminating all elements in $B - A$. If $v(a) \geq v^*$, then a is the first satisfactory element in $L(B, O)$ and is also the first satisfactory element in $L(A, O)$. Thus, a is chosen from A. If all elements in B are unsatisfactory, then a must be the last element in $L(B, O)$. Since A is a subset of B, all elements in A are unsatisfactory and a is the last element in $L(A, O)$. Thus, a is chosen from A.

Note, however, that even a "small" variation in this scheme can lead to a variation of the procedure such that it no longer satisfies condition α. For example:

Satisficing using two orderings: Let X be a population of university graduates who are potential candidates for a job. Given a set of actual candidates, count their number. If the number is smaller than 5, order them alphabetically. If the number of candidates is above 5, order them by their social security number. Whatever ordering is used, choose the first candidate whose undergraduate average is above 85. If there are none, choose the last student on the list.

Condition α is not satisfied. It may be that a is the first candidate with a satisfactory grade in a long list of students ordered by their social security numbers. Still, a might not be the first candidate with a satisfactory grade on a list of only three of the candidates appearing on the original list when they are ordered alphabetically.

To summarize, the satisficing procedure, though it is stated in a way that seems unrelated to the maximization of a preference relation or utility function, can be described as if the decision maker maximizes a preference relation. I know of no other examples of interesting general schemes for choice procedures that satisfy condition α other than the "rational man" and the satisficing procedures. However, later on, when we discuss consumer theory, we will come across several other appealing examples of demand functions that can be rationalized, though they appear to be unrelated to the maximization of a preference relation.

Psychological Motives Not Included within the Framework

The more modern attack on the standard approach to modeling economic agents comes from psychologists, notably from Amos Tversky and Daniel Kahneman. They have provided us with beautiful examples demonstrating not only that rationality is often violated but that there are systematic reasons for the violation resulting from certain elements within our decision procedures. Here are a few examples of this kind that I find particularly relevant.

Framing

The following experiment (conducted by Tversky and Kahneman (1986)) demonstrates that the way in which alternatives are framed may affect decision makers' choices. Subjects were asked to imagine being confronted by the following choice problem:

An outbreak of disease is expected to cause 600 deaths in the United States. Two mutually exclusive programs are expected to yield the following results:

a. 400 people will die.
b. With probability 1/3, 0 people will die, and with probability 2/3, 600 people will die.

In the original experiment, a different group of subjects was given the same background information and asked to choose from the following alternatives:

c. 200 people will be saved.
d. With probability 1/3, all 600 will be saved, and with probability 2/3, none will be saved.

Whereas 78% of the first group chose b, only 28% of the second group chose d. These are "problematic" results since by any reasonable criterion a and c are identical alternatives, as are b and d. Thus, the choice from $\{a, b\}$ should be consistent with the choice from $\{c, d\}$.

Both questions were presented in the above order to 1,200 students taking game theory courses with the result that 73% chose b and 49% chose d. It seems plausible that many students kept in mind their answer to the first question while responding to the second one, and therefore the level of inconsistency was reduced. Nonetheless, a large proportion of students gave different answers to the two problems, which makes the findings even more problematic.

Overall, the results expose the sensitivity of choice to the framing of the alternatives. What is more basic to rational decision making than taking the same choice when only the manner in which the problems are stated is different?

Simplifying the Choice Problem and the Use of Similarities

The following experiment was also conducted by Tversky and Kahneman. One group of subjects was presented with the following choice problem:

Choose one of the two roulette games a or b. Your prize is the one corresponding to the outcome of the chosen roulette game as specified in the following tables:

	Color	White	Red	Green	Yellow
(a)	Chance %	90	6	1	3
	Prize $	0	45	30	−15

	Color	White	Red	Green	Yellow
(b)	Chance %	90	7	1	2
	Prize $	0	45	−10	−15

A different group of subjects was presented the same background information and asked to choose between:

	Color	White	Red	Green	Blue	Yellow
(c)	Chance %	90	6	1	1	2
	Prize $	0	45	30	−15	−15

and

	Color	White	Red	Green	Blue	Yellow
(d)	Chance %	90	6	1	1	2
	Prize $	0	45	45	−10	−15

In the original experiment, 58% of the subjects in the first group chose a, whereas nobody in the second group chose c. When the two problems were presented, one after the other, to about $1,350$ students, 52% chose a and 7% chose c. Interestingly, the median response time among the students who answered a was 53 seconds, whereas the median response time of the students who answered b was 90 seconds.

The results demonstrate a common procedure people practice when confronted with a complicated choice problem. We often transfer the complicated problem into a simpler one by "canceling" similar elements. Although d clearly dominates c, the comparison between a and b is not as easy. Many subjects "cancel" the probabilities of White, Yellow, and Red and are left with comparing the prizes of Green, a process that leads them to choose a.

Incidentally, several times in the past when I presented these choice problems in class, I have had students (some of the best students, in fact) who chose c. They explained that they identified the second problem with the first and used the procedural rule: "I chose a from $\{a, b\}$. The alternatives c and d are identical to the alternatives a and b, respectively. It is only natural then, that I choose c from $\{c, d\}$". This observation brings to our attention the fact that the model of rational man does not allow dependence of choice from B on the previous choices made by the decision maker.

Reason-Based Choice

Making choices sometimes involves finding reasons to pick one alternative over the others. When the deliberation involves the use of reasons strongly associated with the problem at hand ("internal reasons"), we often find it difficult to reconcile the choice with the rational man paradigm.

Imagine, for example, a European student who would choose *Princeton* if allowed to choose from *Princeton, LSE* and would choose *LSE* if he had to choose from *Princeton, Chicago, LSE*. His explanation is that he prefers an American university so long as he does not have to choose between American schools – a choice he deems harder. Having to choose from {*Princeton, Chicago, LSE*}, he finds it difficult deciding between *Princeton* and *Chicago* and therefore chooses not to cross the Atlantic. His choice does not satisfy condition α, not because of a careless specification of the alternatives (as in the restaurant's menu example discussed previously), but because his reasoning involves an attempt to avoid the difficulty of making a decision.

A better example was suggested to me by a student Federico Filippini: "Imagine there's a handsome guy called Albert, who is looking for a date to take to a party. Albert knows two girls that are crazy about him, both of whom would love to go to the party. The two girls are called Mary and Laura. Of the two, Albert prefers Mary. Now imagine that Mary has a sister, and this sister is also crazy about Albert. Albert must now choose between the three girls, Mary, Mary's sister, and Laura. With this third option, I bet that if Albert is rational, he will be taking Laura to the party."

Another example follows Huber, Payne, and Puto (1982):

Let $a = (a_1, a_2)$ be "a holiday package of a_1 days in Paris and a_2 days in London". Choose one of the four vectors $a = (7, 4)$, $b = (4, 7)$, $c = (6, 3)$, and $d = (3, 6)$.

All subjects in the experiment agreed that a day in Paris and a day in London are desirable goods. Some of the subjects were requested to choose between the three alternatives a, b, and c; others had to choose between a, b, and d. The subjects exhibited a clear tendency toward choosing a out of the set $\{a, b, c\}$ and choosing b out of the set $\{a, b, d\}$.

A related experiment is reported in Shafir, Simonson, and Tversky (1993). A group of subjects was asked to imagine having to choose between a camera priced $170 and a better camera, by the same producer, which costs $240. Another group of subjects was asked to imagine having to choose between three cameras – the two described above and a third, much more sophisticated camera, priced at $470. The addition of the third alternative significantly increased the proportion of subjects who chose the $240 camera. The commonsense explanation for this choice is that subjects faced a conflict between two desires, to buy a better camera and to pay less. They resolved the conflict by choosing the "compromise alternative".

To conclude, decision makers look for reasons to prefer one alternative over the other. Typically, making decisions by using "external reasons" (which do not refer to the properties of the choice set) will not cause violations of rationality. However, applying "internal reasons" such as "I prefer the alternative a over the alternative b since a clearly dominates the other alternative c while b does not" might cause conflicts with condition α.

Mental Accounting

The following intuitive example is taken from Kahneman and Tversky (1984). Members of one group of subjects were presented with the following question:

1. Imagine that you have decided to see a play and paid the admission price of $10 per ticket. As you enter the theater, you discover that you have lost the ticket. The seat was not marked and the ticket cannot be recovered. Would you pay $10 for another ticket?

Members of another group were asked to answer the following question:

2. Imagine that you have decided to see a play where the admission is $10 per ticket. As you arrive at the theater, you discover that you have lost a $10 bill. Would you still pay $10 for a ticket for the play?

If the rational man cares only about seeing the play and his wealth, he should realize that there is no difference between the consequence of replying Yes to question 1 and replying Yes to question 2 (in both cases he will own a ticket and will be poorer by $20). Similarly, there is no difference between the consequence of replying No to question 1 and replying No to question 2. Thus, the rational man should give the same answer to both questions. Nonetheless, only 46% said they would buy another ticket after they had lost the first one, whereas 88% said they would buy a ticket after losing the banknote. In the data I collected (among 1,200 subjects) the gap is much smaller: 64% and 80%, accordingly. It is likely that in this case subjects have conducted a calculation where they compared the "mental price" of a ticket to its subjective value. Many of those who decided not to buy another ticket after losing the first one attributed a price of $20 to the ticket rather than $10. This example demonstrates that decision makers may conduct "mental calculations" that are inconsistent with rationality.

Modeling Choice Procedures

There is a large body of evidence showing that decision makers systematically use procedures of choice that violate the classical assumptions and that the rational man paradigm is lacking. The accumulated evidence has had an effect on the development of economic theory, and in recent years we have seen the introduction of more and more economic models in which economic agents are assumed to follow alternative procedures of choice. In this section, we focus on one particular line of research that attempts to incorporate such decision makers into economic models.

Classical models have characterized economic agents using a choice function. The statement $c(A) = a$ means that the decision maker selects a when choosing from the set of alternatives A. We are about to enrich the concept of a choice problem such that it will include not only the set of alternatives but additional information as well. This additional information is considered to be irrelevant to the interests of the decision maker but may nevertheless affect his choice. Here, we will be dealing with a case in which the additional information consists of a *default option*. The statement $c(A, a) = b$ means that when facing the choice problem A with a default alternative a the decision maker chooses the alternative b. Experimental evidence and introspection tell us that a default option is often viewed positively by decision makers, a phenomenon known as the *status quo bias*, which will play a role in the following discussion.

Let X be a finite set of alternatives. Define an *extended choice function* to be a function that assigns a unique element in A to every pair (A, a) where $A \subseteq X$ and $a \in A$.

A *default bias procedure* is an extended choice function characterized by a utility function u and a "bias function" b, which assigns a non-negative number to each alternative. The function u is interpreted as representing the "true" preferences. The number $b(x)$ is interpreted as the bonus attached to x when it is a default alternative. Given an extended choice problem (A, a), the procedure denoted by $DBP_{u,b}$, selects:

$$DBP_{u,b}(A, a) = \begin{cases} x \in A - \{a\} & if \quad u(x) > u(a) + b(a) \ and \ u(x) > u(y) \\ & for \ any \ y \in A - \{a, x\} \\ a & if \quad u(a) + b(a) > u(x), \forall x \in A - \{a\} \end{cases}.$$

Our aim is to characterize the set of extended choice functions that can be described as $DBP_{u,b}$ for some u and b. We will adopt two assumptions:

The Weak Axiom (WA)

We say that an extended choice function c satisfies the Weak Axiom if there are no sets A and B, $a, b \in A \cap B$, $a \neq b$ and $x, y \notin \{a, b\}$ (x and y are not necessarily distinct) such that:

1. $c(A, a) = a$ and $c(B, a) = b$ or
2. $c(A, x) = a$ and $c(B, y) = b$.

The Weak Axiom states that:

1. If a is revealed to be better than b in a choice problem where a is the default, then there cannot be any choice problem in which b is revealed to be better than a when a is the default.
2. If a is revealed to be better than b in a choice problem where neither a nor b is a default, there cannot be any choice problem in which b is revealed to be better than a when again neither a nor b is the default.

Comment:

WA implies that for every a there is a preference relation $\succ_a$ such that $c(A, a)$ is the $\succ_a$-maximal element in A. To see this let

$Y_a = \{x| \ x \neq a$ and there exists a set B such that $c(B, a) = x\}$.

Consider the choice function on the grand set Y_a defined by $D(Y) = c(Y \cup \{a\}, a)$ for any $Y \subseteq Y_a$. By applying WA regarding the extended choice function c, the choice function D on Y_a satisfies condition α, and thus there is an ordering $\succ_a$ on Y_a such that $D(Y)$ is the $\succ_a$-maximum in Y. Extend $\succ_a$ so that a will be just below all the elements in Y_a

and above all elements outside Y_a, which can be ordered in any way, to obtain the conclusion.

Default Tendency (DT)
If $c(A, x) = a$, then $c(A, a) = a$.

The second assumption states that if the decision maker chooses a from a set A when $x \neq a$ is the default, he does not change his mind if x is replaced by a as the default alternative.

Proposition:
An extended choice function c satisfies WA and DT if and only if it is a default-bias procedure.

Proof:
Consider a default-bias procedure c characterized by the functions u and b. It satisfies:

DT: if $c(A, x) = a$ and $x \neq a$, then $u(a) > u(y)$ for any $y \neq a$ in A. Thus, also $u(a) + b(a) > u(y)$ for any $y \neq a$ in A and $c(A, a) = a$.

WA: for any two sets A, B, $a, b \in A \cap B$, $a \neq b$, 1. if $c(A, a) = a$ and $c(B, a) = b$, then we would have both $u(a) + b(a) > u(b)$ and $u(b) > u(a) + b(a)$; and

2. if $c(A, x) = a$ and $c(B, y) = b$ ($x, y \notin \{a, b\}$), then we would have both $u(a) > u(b)$ and $u(b) > u(a)$.

In the other direction, let c be an extended choice function satisfying WA and DT. Define a relation $\succ$ on $X \times \{0, 1\}$ as follows:

- For any pair (A, x) for which $c(A, x) = x$, define $(x, 1) \succ (y, 0)$ for all $y \in A - \{x\}$.
- For any pair (A, x) for which $c(A, x) = y \neq x$, define $(y, 0) \succ (x, 1)$ and $(y, 0) \succ (z, 0)$ for all $z \in A - \{x, y\}$.
- Extend the relation so that $(x, 1) \succ (x, 0)$ for all $x \in X$.

The relation is not necessarily complete or transitive, but by WA it is asymmetric. We will see that $\succ$ can be extended to a full ordering over $X \times \{0, 1\}$ denoted by $\succ^*$. Using problem 4 in Problem Set 1, we only need to show that the relation does not have cycles.

Assume that $\succ$ has a cycle and consider a shortest cycle. By WA there is no cycle of length two, and thus the shortest cycle has to be at least of length three. Steps (a) and (b) establish that it is impossible that the shortest cycle will contain a consecutive pair $(x, 0) \succ (y, 0)$.

a. Assume that the cycle contains a consecutive segment $(x,0) \succ$ $(y,0) \succ (z,1)$.

   If $z = x$, we obtain a contradiction to DT: $((x,0) \succ (y,0)$ implies that there is a set A containing x and y and a third alternative a such that $c(A,a) = x$. Then, also $c(A,x) = x$ and $(x,1) \succ (y,0)$.)

   If $z \neq x$, then there is a set A such that $c(A,z) = y$. Since $(x,0) \succ (y,0)$, $c(A \cup \{x\}, z) = x$ and $(x,0) \succ (z,1)$. Thus, we can shorten the cycle.

b. Assume that the cycle contains a consecutive segment of the type $(x,0) \succ (y,0) \succ (z,0)$. By WA, the three elements are distinct. Since $(y,0) \succ (z,0)$, there exists a set A containing y and z and $a \in A$ such that $c(A,a) = y$. If $a \neq x$, then $c(A \cup \{x\}, a) = x$ and $(x,0) \succ (z,0)$, allowing us to shorten the cycle. If $a = x$, that is, if $c(A,x) = y$, then $(x,0) \succ (y,0) \succ (x,1)$, thus contradicting DT.

It remains to show that it is impossible for the shortest cycle to contain a consecutive segment of the following types:

c. $(x,0) \succ (y,1) \succ (z,0)$ and $y \neq z$. If this were the case, then $c(\{x,y,z\},y) = x$ and $(x,0) \succ (z,0)$, thus allowing us to shorten the cycle.

d. $(x,0) \succ (y,1) \succ (y,0) \succ (z,1)$. By DT $z \neq x$ and by definition $z \neq y$. Consider $c\{\{x,y,z\},z\}$. By WA and $(y,0) \succ (z,1)$ it cannot be z. If it is x, then $(x,0) \succ (y,0)$ and we can shorten the cycle. If it is y, then $(y,0) \succ (x,0)$ and we can shorten the cycle.

We can conclude that $\succ$ does not have a cycle.

Now, let v be a utility function representing $\succ^*$. Define $u(x) = v(x,0)$ and $b(x) = v(x,1) - v(x,0)$ to obtain the result.

1. If $c(A,a) = a$, then $(a,1) \succ (x,0)$ for all $x \in A - \{a\}$ and thus $u(a) + b(a) > u(x)$ for all x, that is, $c(A,a) = DBP_{u,b}(A,a)$.

2. If $c(A,a) = x$, then $(x,0) \succ (a,1)$ and $(x,0) \succ (y,0)$ for all $y \in A - \{a,x\}$ and therefore $u(x) > u(a) + b(a)$ and $u(x) > u(y)$ for all $y \in A - \{a,x\}$. Thus, $c(A,a) = DBP_{u,b}(A,a)$.

Comments on the Significance of Axiomatization

1. There is something aesthetically attractive about the axiomatization, however, I doubt that such an axiomatization is necessary in order for an economist to develop a model in which the procedure will appear. As with other conventions in the profession, this

practice appears to be a barrier to entry that places an unnecessary burden on researchers.

2. A necessary condition for an axiomatization of this type to be of importance is (in my opinion) that we can come up with examples of sensible procedures of choice that satisfy the axioms and are not specified explicitly in the language of the procedure we are axiomatizing. Can you find such a procedure for the above axiomatization? I am unable to. Indeed, many of the axiomatizations in this field lack such examples, and thus, in spite of their aesthetic value, I find them to be futile exercises.

Bibliographic Notes

Recommended readings. Kreps 1990, 24–30; Mas-Colell et al. 1995, chapter 1 C, D.

An excellent book on the lecture's subject is Kreps (1988). For the sources of consistency in choice and revealed preference assumptions, see Samuelson (1948), Houthakker (1950), and Richter (1966). Simon (1955) is the source of the discussion of satisficing. For a discussion of the bounded rationality approach to choice, see Rubinstein (1998). Sen (1993) provides a more philosophical discussion of the subject of this chapter. An excellent introduction to the Dutch Books arguments is Yaari (1985). Kahneman and Tversky (2000) is a definitive textbook on the psychological criticism of the economic approach to rationality. Rabin (1998) surveys the modern economics and psychology approach. The DBP procedure was studied by Massatliglu and Ok (2005). Here we have followed a simpler axiomatization due to Rubinstein and Salant (2006b).

Problem Set 3

Problem 1. (*Easy*)
The following are descriptions of decision-making procedures. Discuss whether the procedures can be described in the framework of the choice model discussed in this lecture and whether they are compatible with the "rational man" paradigm.

   a. The decision maker has in mind a ranking of all alternatives and chooses the alternative that is the worst according to this ranking.
   b. The decision maker chooses an alternative in order to maximize another person's suffering.
   c. The decision maker asks his two children to rank the alternatives and then chooses the alternative that is the best on average.
   d. The decision maker has an ideal point in mind and chooses the alternative that is closest to it.
   e. The decision maker looks for the alternative that appears most often in the choice set.
   f. The decision maker always selects the first alternative that comes to his attention.
   g. The decision maker has an ordering in mind and always chooses the median element.

Problem 2. (*Moderately difficult*)
Let's say that you are to make a choice from a set A. Consider two procedures: (a) You choose from the entire set or (b) You first partition A into the subsets A_1 and A_2, then make a selection from each of the subsets, and finally make a choice from the two selected elements.

   a. Formulate a "path independence" property (for single-valued choice functions).
   b. Show that the rational decision maker satisfies the property.
   c. Find examples of choice procedures that do not satisfy this property.
   d. Show that if a choice function satisfies path independence, then it is consistent with rationality.
   e. Find an example of a choice correspondence satisfying path independence that cannot be rationalized.

Problem 3. (*Easy*)

Let X be a finite set. Check whether the following three choice correspondences satisfy WA:

$C(A) = \{x \in A|$ *the number of* $y \in X$ *for which* $V(x) \geq V(y)$ *is at least* $|X|/2\}$, and if the set is empty, then $C(A) = A$.

$D(A) = \{x \in A|$ *the number of* $y \in A$ *for which* $V(x) \geq V(y)$ *is at least* $|A|/2\}$.

$E(A) = \{x \in A|x \succ_1 y$ *for every* $y \in A$ *or* $x \succ_2 y$ *for every* $y \in A\}$ where $\succ_1$ and $\succ_2$ are two orderings over X.

Problem 4. (*Moderately difficult*)

Consider the following choice procedure: A decision maker has a strict ordering $\succsim$ over the set X and assigns to each $x \in X$ a natural number $class(x)$ to be interpreted as the "class" of x. Given a choice problem A, he chooses the best element in A from those belonging to the most common class in A (i.e., the class that appears in A most often). If there is more than one most common class, he picks the best element from the members of A that belong to a most common class with the highest class number.

   a. Is the procedure consistent with the "rational man" paradigm?
   b. Define the relation: xPy if x is chosen from $\{x, y\}$. Show that the relation P is a strict ordering (complete, asymmetric, and transitive).

Problem 5. (*Moderately difficult. Based on Kalai, Rubinstein, and Spiegler (2002).*)

Consider the following two choice procedures. Explain the procedures and try to persuade a skeptic that they "make sense". Determine for each of them whether they are consistent with the rational man model.

   a. The primitives of the procedure are two numerical (one-to-one) functions u and v defined on X and a number v^*. For any given choice problem A, let $a^* \in A$ be the maximizer of u over A and let b^* be the maximizer of v over A. The decision maker chooses a^* if $v(a^*) \geq v^*$ and b^* if $v(a^*) < v^*$.
   b. The primitives of the procedure are two numerical (one-to-one) functions u and v defined on X and a number u^*. For any given choice problem A, the decision maker chooses the element $a^* \in A$ that maximizes u if $u(a^*) \geq u^*$, and the element $b^* \in A$ that maximizes v if $u(a^*) < u^*$.

Problem 6. (*Moderately difficult. Based on Rubinstein and Salant (2006a).*)

The standard economic choice model assumes that choice is made from a *set*. Let us construct a model where the choice is assumed to be made from a *list*. (Note that the list $< a, b >$ is distinct from $< a, a, b >$ and $< b, a >$.)

Let X be a finite grand set. A *list* is a nonempty finite vector of elements in X. In this problem, consider a *choice function* C to be a function that assigns a single element from $\{a_1, \ldots, a_K\}$ to each vector $L = < a_1, \ldots, a_K >$.

Let $< L_1, \ldots, L_m >$ be the concatenation of the m lists $L_1, \ldots, L_m$ (note that if the length of L_i is k_i, the length of the concatenation is $\Sigma_{i=1,\ldots,m} k_i$). We say that L' *extends* the list L if there is a list M such that $L' =< L, M >$.

We say that a choice function C satisfies Property I if for all $L_1, \ldots, L_m$, $C(< L_1, \ldots, L_m >) = C(< C(L_1), \ldots, C(L_m) >)$.

  a. Interpret Property I. Give two examples of choice functions that satisfy I and two examples that do not.
  b. Define formally the following two properties of a choice function:
     Order Invariance: A change in the order of the elements in the list does not alter the choice.
     Duplication Invariance: Deleting an element that appears elsewhere in the list does not change the choice.
  c. Characterize the choice functions that satisfy the following three properties together: Order Invariance, Duplication Invariance, and property I.

Assume now that at the back of the decision maker's mind there is a value function u defined on the set X (such that $u(x) \neq u(y)$ for all $x \neq y$). For any choice function C, define $v_C(L) = u(C(L))$.

We say that C *accommodates a longer list* if, whenever L' extends L, $v_C(L') \geq v_C(L)$ and there is a pair of lists L' and L such that L' extends L and $v_C(L') > v_C(L)$.

  d. Give two interesting examples of choice functions that accommodate a longer list.
  e. Give two interesting examples of choice functions that satisfy property I but do not accommodate a longer list.

Problem 7. (*Difficult. Based on Rubinstein and Salant (2006a).*)

We say that a choice function c is *lexicographically rational* if there exists a profile of preference relations $\{\succ_a\}_{a \in X}$ (not necessarily distinct) and an ordering O over X such that for every set $A \subset X$, $c(A)$ is the $\succ_a$-maximal element in A, where a is the O-maximal element in A.

A decision maker who follows this procedure is attracted by the most notable element in the set (as described by O). If a is that element, he applies the ordering $\succ_a$ and chooses the $\succ_a$-best element in the set.

We say that c satisfies the *reference point property* if, for every set A, there exists $a \in A$ such that if $a \in A'' \subset A' \subset A$ and $c(A') \in A''$, then $c(A'') = c(A')$.

  a. Show that a choice function c is lexicographically rational if and only if it satisfies the *reference point property*.
  b. Try to come up with a procedure satisfying the reference point axiom that is not stated explicitly in the language of the lexicographically rational choice function (no idea about the answer).

Problem 8. (*Difficult. Based on Cherepanov, Fedderson, and Sandroni (2008).*)
Consider a decision maker who has in mind a set of rationales and a preference
relation and chooses the best alternative that he can rationalize.

Formally, we say that a choice function c is *rationalized* if there is an asymmetric complete relation $\succ$ (*not* necessarily transitive!) and a set of partial
orderings (asymmetric and transitive) $\{\succ_k\}_{k=1...K}$ (called rationales) such
that $c(A)$ is the $\succ$-maximal alternative from among those alternatives found
to be maximal in A by at least one rationale (given a binary relation $\succ$ we say
that x is $\succ$-maximal in A if $x \succ y$ for all $y \in A$). Assume that the relations
are such that the procedure always leads to a solution.

We say that a choice function c satisfies *The Weak Weak Axiom of Revealed Preference (WWARP)* if for all $\{x, y\} \subset B_1 \subset B_2$ $(x \neq y)$ and $c\{x, y\} =
c(B_2) = x$, then $c(B_1) \neq y$.

a. Show that a choice function satisfies WWARP if and only if it is rationalized. For the proof, construct rationales, one for each choice problem,
    that are asymmetric binary relations and allow that $\succ$ will not necessarily be transitive.
b. What do you think about the axiomatization?

Consider the "warm-glow" procedure: The decision maker has two orderings
in mind: one moral $\succsim_M$ and one selfish $\succsim_S$. He chooses the most moral
alternative m as long as he doesn't "lose" too much by not choosing the most
selfish alternative. Formally, for every alternative s there is some alternative
$l(s)$ such that if the most selfish alternative is s, then he is willing to choose
m as long as $m \succsim_S l(s)$. If $l(s) \succ_S m$, he chooses s.

The function l satisfies $s \succsim_S l(s)$ and $s \succsim_S s'$ iff $l(s) \succsim_S l(s')$.

c. Show that WWARP is satisfied by this procedure.
d. Show directly that the "warm-glow" procedure is rationalized (in the
    sense of the definition in this problem).

Consumer Preferences

The Consumer's World

Up to this point we have dealt with the basic economic model of rational choice. In this lecture we will discuss a special case of the rational man paradigm: the *consumer*. A consumer is an economic agent who makes choices between available combinations of commodities. As usual, we have a certain image in mind: a lady goes to the marketplace with money in hand and comes back with a bundle of commodities.

As before, we will begin with a discussion of consumer preferences and utility and only then discuss consumer choice. Our first step is to move from an abstract treatment of the set X to a more detailed structure. We take X to be $\mathbb{R}_+^K = \{x = (x_1, \ldots, x_K) |$ for all k, $x_k \geq 0\}$. An element of X is called a *bundle*. A bundle x is interpreted as a combination of K commodities where x_k is the quantity of commodity k.

Given this special interpretation of X, we impose some conditions on the preferences in addition to those assumed for preferences in general. The additional three conditions use the structure of the space X: monotonicity uses the orderings on the axis (the ability to compare bundles by the amount of any particular commodity); continuity uses the topological structure (the ability to talk about closeness); convexity uses the algebraic structure (the ability to speak of the sum of two bundles and the multiplication of a bundle by a scalar). It will be useful to demonstrate properties of the consumer's preferences by referring to the map of indifference curves, where an indifference curve is a set of the type $\{y | y \sim x\}$ for some bundle x (see problem 1 in Problem Set 1).

Monotonicity

Monotonicity is a property that gives commodities the meaning of "goods". It is the condition that more is better. Increasing the amount of some commodities cannot hurt, and increasing the amount of all commodities is strictly desired. Formally,

Monotonicity

The relation $\succsim$ satisfies *monotonicity at the bundle y* if for all $x \in X$,

if $x_k \geq y_k$ for all k, then $x \succsim y$, and
if $x_k > y_k$ for all k, then $x \succ y$.

The relation $\succsim$ satisfies *monotonicity* if it satisfies monotonicity at every $y \in X$.

In some cases, we will further assume that the consumer is strictly happier with any additional quantity of any commodity.

Strong Monotonicity

The relation $\succsim$ satisfies *strong monotonicity at the bundle y* if for all $x \in X$

if $x_k \geq y_k$ for all k and $x \neq y$, then $x \succ y$.

The relation $\succsim$ satisfies *strong monotonicity* if it satisfies strong monotonicity at every $y \in X$.

Of course, in the case that preferences are represented by a utility function, preferences satisfying monotonicity (or strong monotonicity) are represented by monotonic increasing (or strong monotonic increasing) utility functions.

Examples:

- The preferences represented by $min\{x_1, x_2\}$ satisfy *monotonicity* but not *strong monotonicity*.
- The preferences represented by $x_1 + x_2$ satisfy *strong monotonicity*.
- Denote by $d(x, y) = \sqrt{\sum(x_k - y_k)^2}$ the standard distance function on the Euclidean space. A property related to monotonicity that is sometimes used in the literature is called nonsatiation. A preference is said to be *nonsatiated at the bundle y* if for any $\varepsilon > 0$ there is some $x \in X$ that is less than ε away from y so that $x \succ y$. The preference relation represented by $u(x) = -d(x, x^*)$ does not satisfy monotonicity but is nonsatiated at every bundle except x^*. Every preference relation that is monotonic at a bundle y is also nonsatiated at y, but the reverse is, of course, not true.

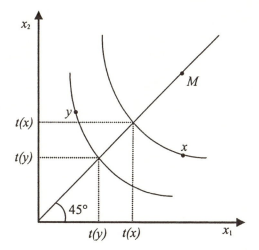

Figure 4.1
Construction of the utility function.

Continuity

We will use the topological structure of $\mathbb{R}_+^K$ (with the standard distance function d, defined above) to apply the definition of continuity discussed in Lecture 2. We say that the preferences $\succsim$ satisfy *continuity* if for all $a, b \in X$, $a \succ b$ implies that there is an $\varepsilon > 0$ such that $x \succ y$ for any x and y such that $d(x, a) < \varepsilon$ and $d(y, b) < \varepsilon$.

Existence of a Utility Representation

Debreu's theorem guarantees that any continuous preference relation is represented by some (continuous) utility function. If we assume monotonicity as well, we then have a simple and elegant proof:

Claim:

Any consumer preference relation satisfying monotonicity and continuity can be represented by a utility function.

Proof:

Let us first show that for every bundle x, there is a bundle on the main diagonal (having equal quantities of all commodities), such that the consumer is indifferent between that bundle and the bundle x. (See fig. 4.1.) The bundle x is at least as good as the bundle $0 = (0, \ldots, 0)$. On the other hand, the bundle $M = (max_k\{x_k\}, \ldots, max_k\{x_k\})$ is at least as good as x. Both 0 and M are on the main diagonal. By continuity, there is a bundle on the main diagonal that is indifferent to x (see Problem Set 2). By monotonicity this bundle is unique; we will denote it by $(t(x), \ldots, t(x))$. Let $u(x) = t(x)$. To see that the function u represents the preferences, note that by transitivity of the preferences $x \succsim y$ iff $(t(x), \ldots, t(x)) \succsim (t(y), \ldots, t(y))$, and by *monotonicity* this is true iff $t(x) \geq t(y)$.

Convexity

Consider, for example, a scenario in which the alternatives are candidates for some political post. The candidates are positioned in a left-right array as follows:

$$—a—\text{-}b—\quad c—\quad d—\quad\text{-}e—.$$

Under normal circumstances, if we know that a voter prefers b to d, then we tend to conclude that:

- he prefers c to d, but not necessarily a to d (the candidate a may be too extreme).
- he prefers d to e (namely, we do not find it plausible that he views moving both right and left as improvements upon d).

The notion of convex preferences captures two similar intuitions that are suitable for situations where there exists a "geography" of the set of alternatives in the sense that we can talk about one alternative being between two others:

- If x is preferred to y, then going part of the way from y to x is also an improvement upon y.
- If z is between x and y, then it is impossible that both x and y are better than z.

Convexity is appropriate for a situation in which the argument "if a move is an improvement, so is any move part of the way" is legitimate, whereas the argument "if a move is harmful, then so is a move part of the way" is not.

Following are two formalizations of these two intuitions.

Convexity 1:

The preference relation $\succsim$ satisfies *convexity 1* if $x \succsim y$ and $\alpha \in (0, 1)$ implies that $\alpha x + (1 - \alpha) y \succsim y$ (fig. 4.2).

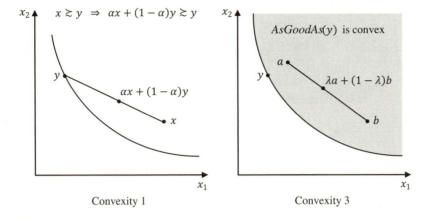

Figure 4.2
Two definitions of convexity.

Convexity 2:
The preference relation $\succsim$ satisfies *convexity 2* if for all x, y, and z such that $z = \alpha x + (1 - \alpha)y$ for some $\alpha \in (0, 1)$, either $z \succsim x$ or $z \succsim y$.

Another definition of convexity, which uses the notion of a convex set, follows. Recall that a set A is convex if for all $a, b \in A$ and for all $\lambda \in [0, 1]$, $\lambda a + (1 - \lambda)b \in A$.

Convexity 3:
The preference relation $\succsim$ satisfies *convexity 3* if for all y the set $AsGoodAs(y) = \{z \in X \,|\, z \succsim y\}$ is convex (fig. 4.2).

This captures the intuition that if both z_1 and z_2 are better than y, then the average of z_1 and z_2 is definitely better than y.

We proceed to show that the three definitions are equivalent.

Claim:
If the preference relation $\succsim$ satisfies one of the conditions convexity 1, convexity 2, or convexity 3, it satisfies the other two.

Proof:
Assume that $\succsim$ satisfies convexity 1 and let $x, y, z \in X$ such that $z = \alpha x + (1 - \alpha)y$ for some $\alpha \in (0, 1)$. Without loss of generality, assume $x \succsim y$. By convexity 1 we have $z \succsim y$. Thus, $\succsim$ satisfies convexity 2.

Assume that $\succsim$ satisfies convexity 2 and let $z, z' \in AsGoodAs(y)$. Then, by convexity 2, $\alpha z + (1 - \alpha)z'$ is at least as good as either z or z' (or both). In any case, by transitivity, $\alpha z + (1 - \alpha)z' \succsim y$, that is, $\alpha z + (1 - \alpha)z' \in AsGoodAs(y)$, and thus $\succsim$ satisfies convexity 3.

Assume that $\succsim$ satisfies convexity 3. If $x \succsim y$, then both x and y are in $AsGoodAs(y)$ and thus $\alpha x + (1 - \alpha)y \in AsGoodAs(y)$, which means that $\alpha x + (1 - \alpha)y \succsim y$. Thus, $\succsim$ satisfies convexity 1.

Convexity also has a stronger version:

Strict Convexity

The preference relation $\succsim$ satisfies *strict convexity* if $a \succsim y$, $b \succsim y$, $a \neq b$, and $\lambda \in (0, 1)$ imply that $\lambda a + (1 - \lambda)b \succ y$.

Examples:

The preferences represented by $\sqrt{x_1} + \sqrt{x_2}$ satisfy strict convexity. The preference relations represented by $min\{x_1, x_2\}$ and $x_1 + x_2$ satisfy convexity but not strict convexity. The lexicographic preferences satisfy strict convexity. The preferences represented by $x_1^2 + x_2^2$ do not satisfy convexity.

We now look at the properties of the utility representations of convex preferences.

Quasi-Concavity

A function u is *quasi-concave* if for all y the set $\{x|\, u(x) \geq u(y)\}$ is convex.

The notion of quasi-concavity is similar to concavity in that for any function f that is either quasi-concave or concave, the set $\{x|f(x) \geq f(y)\}$ is convex for any y. (Recall that u is *concave* if for all x, y, and $\lambda \in [0, 1]$ we have $u(\lambda x + (1 - \lambda)y) \geq \lambda u(x) + (1 - \lambda)u(y)$.)

Obviously, if a preference relation is represented by a utility function, then it is convex iff the utility function is quasi-concave. However, the convexity of $\succsim$ does not imply that a utility function representing $\succsim$ is concave. Furthermore, there are examples of continuous and convex preferences that do not have a utility representation by any concave function.

Special Classes of Preferences

Usually in economics, we discuss a consumer with some variations of monotonicity, continuity, and convexity. We will refer to such a

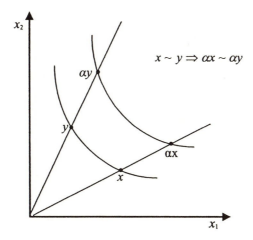

Figure 4.3
Homothetic preferences.

consumer as a "classical consumer". Often, we assume that the consumer possesses preferences belonging to a narrower class, characterized by additional special properties. Following are some examples of "popular" classes of preference relations discussed in the literature.

The Class of Homothetic Preferences

A preference $\succsim$ is *homothetic* if $x \succsim y$ implies $\alpha x \succsim \alpha y$ for all $\alpha \geq 0$. (See fig. 4.3.)

The preferences represented by $\Pi_{k=1,\ldots,K} x_k^{\beta_k}$, where β_k is positive, are homothetic. More generally, any preference relation represented by a utility function u that is homogeneous of any degree λ (that is $u(\alpha x) = \alpha^\lambda u(x)$) is homothetic. This is because $x \succsim y$ iff $u(x) \geq u(y)$ iff $\alpha^\lambda u(x) \geq \alpha^\lambda u(y)$ iff $u(\alpha x) \geq u(\alpha y)$ iff $\alpha x \succsim \alpha y$. Lexicographic preferences are also homothetic.

Claim:

Any homothetic, continuous, and monotonic preference relation on the commodity bundle space can be represented by a continuous utility function that is homogeneous of degree one.

Proof:

We have already proved that any bundle x has a unique bundle $(t(x), \ldots, t(x))$ on the main diagonal so that $x \sim (t(x), \ldots, t(x))$, and that the function $u(x) = t(x)$ represents $\succsim$. By the assumption that the

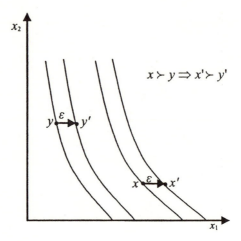

Figure 4.4
Quasi-linear (in good 1) preferences.

preferences are homothetic, $\alpha x \sim (\alpha t(x), \ldots, \alpha t(x))$ and thus $u(\alpha x) = \alpha t(x) = \alpha u(x)$. The proof that u is continuous is left as an exercise.

The Class of Quasi-Linear Preferences

A preference is *quasi-linear* in commodity 1 (referred to as the "numeraire") if $x \succsim y$ implies $(x + \varepsilon e_1) \succsim (y + \varepsilon e_1)$ (where $e_1 = (1, 0, \ldots, 0)$ and $\varepsilon > 0$). (See fig. 4.4.)

The indifference curves of preferences that are quasi-linear in commodity 1 are parallel to each other (relative to the first commodity axis). That is, if I is an indifference curve, then the set $I_\varepsilon = \{x \mid \text{there exists } y \in I \text{ such that } x = y + (\varepsilon, 0, \ldots, 0)\}$ is an indifference curve as well. Any preference relation represented by $x_1 + v(x_2, \ldots, x_K)$ for some function v is quasi-linear in commodity 1. Furthermore:

Claim:

Any continuous preference relation satisfying strong monotonicity (at least in commodity 1) and quasi-linearity in commodity 1 can be represented by a utility function of the form $x_1 + v(x_2, \ldots, x_K)$.
For the proof we need the following lemma:

Lemma:

Let $\succsim$ be a preference relation that is monotonic, continuous, quasi-linear, and strongly monotonic in commodity 1. Then, for every

$(x_2, \ldots, x_K)$ there is a number $v(x_2, \ldots, x_K)$ such that $(0, x_2, \ldots, x_K) \sim (v(x_2, \ldots, x_K), 0, \ldots, 0)$.

Proof of the Lemma

The general proof is left to the problem set, but here let's prove the case of $K = 2$.

Let $T = \{t \mid (0, t) \succ (x_1, 0) \text{ for all } x_1\}$. Assume $T \neq \emptyset$ and denote $m = \inf T$. We distinguish between two cases:

(i) $m \in T$. Then $m > 0$ and $(1, m) \succ (0, m)$. By continuity, there is an $\epsilon > 0$ such that $(1, m - \epsilon) \succ (0, m)$, and thus $(1, m - \epsilon) \succ (x_1 + 1, 0)$ for all x_1. Since $m = \inf T$, then there exists an x_1^* such that $(x_1^*, 0) \succsim (0, m - \epsilon)$, and by the quasi-linearity in commodity 1, $(x_1^* + 1, 0) \succsim (1, m - \epsilon)$, a contradiction.

(ii) $m \notin T$. Then $(x_1^*, 0) \sim (0, m)$ for some x_1^*. By the strong monotonicity of commodity 1, $(x_1^* + 1, 0) \succ (0, m)$. By continuity, there is an $\epsilon > 0$ such that $(x_1^* + 1, 0) \succ (0, x_2^*)$, for any $m + \epsilon \geq x_2^* \geq m$, contradicting $m = \inf T$.

Consequently, $T = \emptyset$, and for every x_2 there is an x_1 such that $(x_1, 0) \succsim (0, x_2) \succsim (0, 0)$, and thus by continuity $(v(x_2), 0) \sim (0, x_2)$ for some number $v(x_2)$. This completes the proof of the lemma.

Note that the above claim is incorrect without the quasi-linearity assumption. The utility function $u(x_1, x_2) = x_2 - 1/(x_1 + 1)$ represents strongly monotonic and continuous preferences for which $m = 1$.

Proof of the Claim

By the lemma, for every $(x_2, \ldots, x_K)$ there is a number $v(x_2, \ldots, x_K)$ so that $(v(x_2, \ldots, x_K), 0, \ldots, 0) \sim (0, x_2, \ldots, x_K)$. By the quasi-linearity in commodity 1, $(x_1 + v(x_2, \ldots, x_K), 0, \ldots, 0) \sim (x_1, x_2, \ldots, x_K)$, and thus by strong mono- tonicity in the first commodity, the function $x_1 + v(x_2, \ldots, x_K)$ represents $\succsim$.

Thus, we used the quasi linearity for two purposes. First, we showed that for every bundle x there is a quantity of the first good $u(x)$ such that $x \sim (u(x), 0, \ldots, 0)$. By the strong monotonicity in the first commodity this allows us to use $u(x)$ as a utility function representing the consumer's preferences. Second, the quasi linearity is used to show that this function u has the structure of $x_1 + v(x_2, \ldots, x_K)$.

The above claim shows that any continuous preference relation that is quasi-linear in the first commodity is consistent with a procedure according to which the consumer asks himself what is the value (in terms of the first commodity) of the combination of goods $2 \ldots k$, and that evaluation is independent of the quantity of the first commodity.

Claim:

Any continuous preference relation $\succsim$ on $\mathbb{R}_+^K$ satisfying strong monotonicity and quasi-linearity in all commodities can be represented by a utility function of the form $\sum_{k=1}^K \alpha_k x_k$.

Here I present two proofs for the case of $K = 2$ only. The general proof for any K is left for the problem set.

Proof 1:

Using the previous claim, we have that the preference relation over the bundle space is represented by the function $u(x_1, x_2) = x_1 + v(x_2)$ where $(0, x_2) \sim (v(x_2), 0)$. Let $(0, 1) \sim (c, 0)$.

It is sufficient to show that $v(x_2) = cx_2$.

Assume that for some x_2 we have $v(x_2) > cx_2$ (a similar argument applies for the case $v(x_2) < cx_2$). Choose two integers S and T such that $v(x_2)/c > S/T > x_2$.

Let us note that if $(a, 0) \sim (0, b)$, then all points (ka, lb) for which $k + l = n$ reside on the same indifference curve. The proof is by induction on n. By the inductive step $((n-1)a, 0) \sim ((n-2)a, b)$, and by the quasi-linearity in commodity 1 $(na, 0) \sim ((n-1)a, b)$. By the inductive step for all $j \geq 0$ we have $((n-j-1)a, jb) \sim ((n-j-2)a, (j+1)b)$, and by the quasi-linearity in commodity 1 $((n-j)a, jb) \sim ((n-j-1)a, (j+1)b)$ for all $j \geq 0$.

Thus, $(0, Tx_2) \sim (Tv(x_2), 0)$ and $(0, S) \sim (Sc, 0)$. However, since $S > Tx_2$, we have $(0, Tx_2) \prec (0, S)$, and since $Tv(x_2) > Sc$, we have $(Tv(x_2), 0) \succ (Sc, 0)$, which is a contradiction.

Proof 2:

We will see that $v(a + b) = v(a) + v(b)$ for all a and b. By definition of v, $(0, a) \sim (v(a), 0)$ and $(0, b) \sim (v(b), 0)$. By the quasi-linearity in good 1, $(v(b), a) \sim (v(a) + v(b), 0)$ and by the quasi-linearity of good 2, $(0, a + b) \sim (v(b), a)$. Thus, $(0, a + b) \sim (v(a) + v(b), 0)$ and $v(a + b) = v(a) + v(b)$.

Let $v(1) = c$. Then for any natural numbers m and n we have $v(m/n) = cm/n$. Since $v(0) = 0$ and v is an increasing function, it must be that $v(x) = cx$ for all x.

(The equation $v(a + b) = v(a) + v(b)$ is called Cauchy's functional equation, and without further assumptions, like monotonicity, there are nonlinear functions that satisfy it.)

Differentiable Preferences (and the Use of Derivatives in Economic Theory)

We often assume in microeconomics that utility functions are differentiable and thus use standard calculus to analyze the consumer. In this course I (almost) avoid calculus. This is part of a deliberate attempt to steer you away from a "mechanistic" approach to economic theory.

Can we give the differentiability of a utility function an "economic" interpretation? In this section a nonconventional definition of *differentiable preferences* is introduced. Basically, differentiability of preferences will be taken as the requirement that the directions for improvement can be calculated by "personal local prices".

Let us confine ourselves to preferences satisfying monotonicity and convexity. For any vector x we say that the vector $z \in \mathbb{R}^K$ is an *improvement* if $x + z \succ x$. We say that $d \in \mathbb{R}^K$ is an *improvement direction* at x if any small move from x in the direction of d is an improvement, that is, there is some λ^* such that for all $\lambda^* > \lambda > 0$ the vector λd is an improvement.

Let $D(x)$ be the set of all improvement directions at x. Note that:

1. If $d \in D(x)$, then $\lambda d \in D(x)$.
2. If the preferences are strictly convex, then any improvement is also an improvement direction.
3. If the preferences satisfy strong monotonicity, continuity, and convexity, then any improvement is also an improvement direction. To see it, assume $x + d \succ x$. Take $\lambda^* = 1$. For any $1 > \lambda > 0$ we will show that $x + \lambda d = \lambda(x + d) + (1 - \lambda)x \succ x$. By continuity, there is a vector $z \succ x$ with $z_k \leq (x + d)_k$ for all k and with strict inequality for every k for which $(x + d)_k > 0$. For all k we have $(x + \lambda d)_k \geq (\lambda z + (1 - \lambda)x)_k$ and $x + \lambda d \neq \lambda z + (1 - \lambda)x$. By strong monotonicity, $x + \lambda d \succ \lambda z + (1 - \lambda)x$. Finally, by convexity, $\lambda z + (1 - \lambda)x \succsim x$. Thus, $x + \lambda d \succ x$.
4. Given monotonicity, if $d_k > 0$ for all k, then $d \in D(x)$.

We say that a consumer's preferences $\succsim$ are *differentiable at the bundle* x if there is a vector $v(x)$ of K nonnegative numbers so that $D(x) = \{d \in \mathbb{R}^K \mid dv(x) > 0\}$ ($dv(x)$ is the inner product of the two vectors d

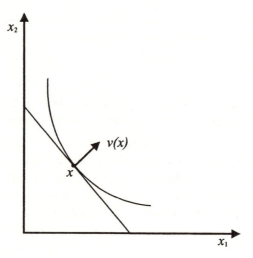

Figure 4.5
Differentiable preferences.

and $v(x)$). The vector of numbers $(v_1(x), \ldots, v_K(x))$ is interpreted as the vector of "subjective values" of the commodities. Starting from x, any small move in a direction that is evaluated by this vector as positive is an improvement. We say that $\succsim$ is *differentiable* if it is differentiable at any bundle x (see fig. 4.5).

Examples:

- The preferences represented by $2x_1 + 3x_2$ are differentiable. At each point x, $v(x) = (2, 3)$.
- The preferences represented by $\min\{x_1, \ldots, x_K\}$ are differentiable only at points where there is a unique commodity k for which $x_k < x_l$ for all $l \neq k$ (verify). For example, at $x = (5, 3, 8, 6), v(x) = (0, 1, 0, 0)$.

Let us see now that when the preferences $\succsim$ are represented by a utility function u that is differentiable with positive partial derivative and quasi-concave, the preferences are differentiable. Most examples of utility functions that are used in the economic literature are differentiable.

Let us add some notation. Given a differentiable utility function u, let $du/dx_k(x)$ be the partial derivative of u with respect to the commodity k at point x. Let $\nabla u(x)$, the gradient, be the vector of these partial derivatives. Recall that the meaning of differentiability of u at a point

x is that the rate of change of u when moving from x at any direction d is $d \cdot \nabla u(x)$. That is, $\lim_{\epsilon \to 0} \frac{u(x+\epsilon d) - u(x)}{\epsilon} = d \cdot \nabla u(x)$.

Now, let $v(x) = \nabla u(x)$. We will show that $D(x) = \{d \in \mathbb{R}^K \mid dv(x) > 0\}$.

We first show that $D(x) \subseteq \{d \in \mathbb{R}^K \mid dv(x) > 0\}$. By contradiction, let $d \in D(x)$ where $d \cdot v(x) \leq 0$. Without loss of generality, let $x + d \succ x$, since otherwise d can be rescaled. Let $e = (1, \ldots, 1)$. By continuity, for all small enough $\epsilon > 0$ we have $x + (d - \epsilon e) \succ x$. By convexity and strong monotonicity of the preferences (which followed from the quasi-concavity and positive partial derivatives of u) $(d - \epsilon e) \in D(x)$. However, $(d - \epsilon e) \cdot v(x) < 0$ and thus by the differentiability of u, for δ small enough, $u(x + \delta(d - \epsilon e)) < u(x)$. A contradiction.

The other direction, $D(x) \supseteq \{d \in \mathbb{R}^K \mid dv(x) > 0\}$, follows immediately from the differentiability of u since $dv(x) > 0$ implies $u(x + \epsilon d) > u(x)$ for ϵ small enough. That is, $d \in D(x)$.

Bibliographic Notes

Recommended readings. Kreps 1990, 32–37; Mas-Colell et al. 1995, chapter 3, A–C.

The material in this lecture up to the discussion of differentiability is fairly standard and closely parallels that found in Arrow and Hahn (1971).

Problem Set 4

Problem 1. (*Easy*)
Consider the preference relations on the interval $[0, 1]$ that are continuous. What can you say about those preferences which are also strictly convex?

Problem 2. (*Standard*)
Show that if the preferences $\succsim$ satisfy continuity and monotonicity, then the function $u(x)$, defined by $x \sim (u(x), \ldots, u(x))$, is continuous.

Problem 3. (*Standard*)
In a world with two commodities, consider the following condition:

The preference relation $\succsim$ satisfies *convexity 4* if for all x and $\varepsilon > 0$

$$(x_1, x_2) \sim (x_1 - \varepsilon, x_2 + \delta_1) \sim (x_1 - 2\varepsilon, x_2 + \delta_1 + \delta_2) \text{ implies } \delta_2 \geq \delta_1.$$

Interpret convexity 4 and show that for strong monotonic and continuous preferences, it is equivalent to the convexity of the preference relation.

Problem 4. (*Standard*)
Complete the proof (for all K) of the claim that any continuous preference relation satisfying strong monotonicity and quasi-linearity in all commodities can be represented by a utility function of the form $\sum_{k=1}^{K} \alpha_k x_k$ where $\alpha_k > 0$ for all k.

Problem 5. (*Difficult*)
Show that for any consumer's preference relation $\succsim$ satisfying continuity, monotonicity, strong monotonicity with respect to commodity 1, and quasi-linearity with respect to commodity 1, there exists a number $v(x)$ such that $x \sim (v(x), 0, \ldots, 0)$ for every vector x.

Problem 6. (*Easy*)
We say that a preference relation satisfies *separability* if it can be represented by an additive utility function, that is, a function of the type $u(x) = \Sigma_k v_k(x_k)$.

a. Show that such preferences satisfy condition S: for any subset of commodities J, and for any bundles a, b, c, d, we have:

$$(a_J, c_{-J}) \succsim (b_J, c_{-J}) \Leftrightarrow (a_J, d_{-J}) \succsim (b_J, d_{-J}),$$

where (x_J, y_{-J}) is the vector that takes the components of x for any $k \in J$ and takes the components of y for any $k \notin J$.

b. Show that for $K = 2$ such preferences satisfy the "Hexagon-condition":
   If $(a, b) \succsim (c, d)$ and $(c, e) \succsim (f, b)$, then $(a, e) \succsim (f, d)$.
c. Give an example of a continuous preference relation that satisfies condition S and does not satisfy separability.

Problem 7. (*Difficult*)

a. Show that the preferences represented by the utility function $min\{x_1, \ldots, x_K\}$ are not differentiable.
b. Check the differentiability of the lexicographic preferences in $\mathbb{R}^2$.
c. Assume that $\succsim$ is monotonic, convex, and differentiable such that for every x we have $D(x) = \{d | (x + d) \succ x\}$. What can you say about $\succsim$?
d. Assume that $\succsim$ is a monotonic, convex, and differentiable preference relation. Let $E(x) = \{d \in \mathbb{R}^K |$ there exists $\varepsilon^* > 0$ such that $x + \varepsilon d \prec x$ for all $\varepsilon \leq \varepsilon^*\}$. Show that $\{-d | d \in D(x)\} \subseteq E(x)$ but not necessarily $\{-d | d \in D(x)\} = E(x)$.
e. Consider the consumer's preferences in a world with two commodities defined by:

$$u(x_1, x_2) = \begin{cases} x_1 + x_2 & if \quad x_1 + x_2 \leq 1 \\ 1 + 2x_1 + x_2 & if \quad x_1 + x_2 > 1 \end{cases}.$$

Show that these preferences are not continuous but nevertheless are differentiable according to our definition.

Demand: Consumer Choice

The Rational Consumer's Choice from a Budget Set

In Lecture 4 we discussed the consumer's preferences. In this lecture we adopt the "rational man" paradigm in discussing consumer choice.

Given a consumer's preference relation $\succsim$ on $X = \mathbb{R}_+^K$, we can talk about his choice from an arbitrary set of bundles. However, since we are laying the foundation for "price models", we are interested in the consumer's choice in a particular class of choice problems called budget sets. A *budget set* is a set of bundles that can be represented as $B(p, w) = \{x \in X \mid px \leq w\}$, where p is a vector of positive numbers (interpreted as prices) and w is a positive number (interpreted as the consumer's wealth).

Obviously, any set $B(p, w)$ is compact (it is closed since it is defined by weak inequalities, and bounded since for any $x \in B(p, w)$ and for all k, $0 \leq x_k \leq w/p_k$). It is also convex since if $x, y \in B(p, w)$, then $px \leq w$, $py \leq w$, $x_k \geq 0$, and $y_k \geq 0$ for all k. Thus, for all $\alpha \in [0, 1]$, $p[\alpha x + (1 - \alpha)y] = \alpha px + (1 - \alpha)py \leq w$ and $\alpha x_k + (1 - \alpha)y_k \geq 0$ for all k, that is, $\alpha x + (1 - \alpha)y \in B(p, w)$.

We will refer to the problem of finding the $\succsim$-best bundle in $B(p, w)$ as the *consumer problem*.

Claim:

If $\succsim$ is a continuous relation, then all consumer problems have a solution.

Proof:

If $\succsim$ is continuous, then it can be represented by a continuous utility function u. By the definition of the term "utility representation", finding an $\succsim$ optimal bundle is equivalent to solving the problem $\max_{x \in B(p,w)} u(x)$. Because the budget set is compact and u is continuous, the problem has a solution.

To emphasize that a utility representation is not necessary for the current analysis and that we could make do with the concept of preferences, let us go through a direct proof of the previous claims, that avoids the notion of utility.

Direct Proof:

For any $x \in B(p,w)$, define the set $Inferior(x) = \{y \in X \mid x \succ y\}$. By the continuity of the preferences, every such set is open. Assume there is no solution to the consumer problem of maximizing $\succsim$ on $B(p,w)$. Then, every $z \in B(p,w)$ is a member of some set $Inferior(x)$, that is, the collection of sets $\{Inferior(x) \mid x \in B(p,w)\}$ covers $B(p,w)$. A collection of open sets that covers a compact set has a finite subset of sets that covers it. Thus, there is a finite collection $Inferior(x^1), \ldots, Inferior(x^n)$ that covers $B(p,w)$. Letting x^j be the optimal bundle within the finite set $\{x^1, \ldots, x^n\}$, we obtain that x^j is an optimal bundle in $B(p,w)$, a contradiction.

Claim:

1. If $\succsim$ is convex, then the set of solutions for a choice from $B(p,w)$ (or any other convex set) is convex.
2. If $\succsim$ is strictly convex, then every consumer problem has at most one solution.

Proof:

1. Assume that both x and y maximize $\succsim$ given $B(p,w)$. By the convexity of the budget set $B(p,w)$, we have $\alpha x + (1-\alpha)y \in B(p,w)$, and by the convexity of the preferences, $\alpha x + (1-\alpha)y \succsim x \succsim z$ for all $z \in B(p,w)$. Thus, $\alpha x + (1-\alpha)y$ is also a solution to the consumer problem.
2. Assume that both x and y (where $x \neq y$) are solutions to the consumer problem $B(p,w)$. Then $x \sim y$ (both are solutions to the same maximization problem) and $\alpha x + (1-\alpha)y \in B(p,w)$ (the budget set is convex). By the strict convexity of $\succsim$, $\alpha x + (1-\alpha)y \succ x$, which is a contradiction of x being a maximal bundle in $B(p,w)$.

The Consumer Problem with Differentiable Preferences

When the preferences are differentiable, we are provided with a "useful" condition for characterizing the optimal solution: the "value per dollar"

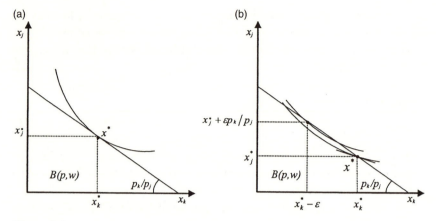

Figure 5.1
(a) x^* is a solution to the consumer problem $B(p, w)$. (b) x^* is not a solution to the consumer problem $B(p, w)$.

at the point x^* of the k'th commodity (which is consumed) must be as large as the "value per dollar" of any other commodity.

Claim:

Assume that the consumer's preferences are differentiable with $v_1(x^*)$, $\ldots, v_K(x^*)$ the "subjective value numbers" (see the definition of differentiable preferences in Lecture 4). If x^* is an optimal bundle in the consumer problem and k is a consumed commodity (i.e., $x_k^* > 0$), then it must be that $v_k(x^*)/p_k \geq v_j(x^*)/p_j$ for all other j.

Proof:

Assume that x^* is a solution to the consumer problem $B(p, w)$ and that $x_k^* > 0$ and $v_j(x^*)/p_j > v_k(x^*)/p_k$ (see fig. 5.1). A "move" in the direction of reducing the consumption of the k'th commodity by 1 and increasing the consumption of the j'th commodity by p_k/p_j is an improvement since $v_j(x^*)p_k/p_j - v_k(x^*) > 0$. As $x_k^* > 0$, we can find $\varepsilon > 0$ small enough such that decreasing k's quantity by ε and increasing j's quantity by $\varepsilon p_k/p_j$ is feasible. This brings the consumer to a strictly better bundle, contradicting the assumption that x^* is a solution to the consumer problem.

Claim:

If x^* is a solution to the consumer problem $B(p, w)$ and both $x_k^* > 0$ and $x_j^* > 0$, then the ratio $v_k(x^*)/v_j(x^*)$ must be equal to the price ratio p_k/p_j.

From the above you can derive the "classic" necessary conditions on the consumer's maximization when the preferences are represented by a differentiable utility function u, with positive partial derivatives, using the equality $v_k(x^*) = \partial u/\partial x_k(x^*)$.

In order to establish sufficient conditions for maximization, we require also that the preferences be convex.

Claim:

If $\succsim$ is strongly monotonic, convex, continuous, and differentiable, and if at x^*

- $px^* = w$,
- for all k such that $x_k^* > 0$, and for any commodity j, $v_k(x^*)/p_k \geq v_j(x^*)/p_j$,

then x^* is a solution to the consumer problem.

Proof:

If x^* is not a solution, then there is a bundle y such that $py \leq px^*$ and $y \succ x^*$. By continuity we can assume that $y_k > 0$ for all k.

Let $\mu = v_k(x^*)/p_k$ for all k with $x_k^* > 0$. Now,

$$0 \geq p(y - x^*) = \sum p_k(y_k - x_k^*) \geq \sum v_k(x^*)(y_k - x_k^*)/\mu$$

since: (1) y is feasible, (2) for a good k with $x_k^* > 0$ we have $p_k = v_k(x^*)/\mu$, and (3) for a good k with $x_k^* = 0$, $(y_k - x_k^*) \geq 0$ and $p_k \geq v_k(x^*)/\mu$. Thus, $0 \geq v(x^*)(y - x^*)$, in contradiction to $(y - x^*)$ being an improvement direction.

The Demand Function

We have arrived at an important stage on the way to developing a market model in which we derive demand from preferences. Assume that the consumer's preferences are such that for any $B(p, w)$, the consumer's problem has a unique solution. Let us denote this solution by $x(p, w)$. The function $x(p, w)$ is called the *demand function*. The domain of the demand function is $\mathbb{R}_{++}^{K+1}$, whereas its range is $\mathbb{R}_+^K$.

Example:

Consider a consumer in a world with two commodities having the following lexicographic preference relation, attaching the first priority to the sum of the quantities of the goods and the second priority to the quantity of commodity 1:

$x \succsim y$ if $x_1 + x_2 > y_1 + y_2$ or both $x_1 + x_2 = y_1 + y_2$ and $x_1 \geq y_1$.

This preference relation is strictly convex but not continuous. It induces the following noncontinuous demand function:

$$x((p_1, p_2), w) = \begin{cases} (0, w/p_2) & if \quad p_2 < p_1 \\ (w/p_1, 0) & if \quad p_2 \geq p_1 \end{cases}.$$

We now turn to studying some properties of the demand function.

Claim:

$x(p, w) = x(\lambda p, \lambda w)$ (i.e., the demand function is *homogeneous of degree zero*).

Proof:

This follows (with no assumptions about the preference relations) from the basic equality $B(\lambda p, \lambda w) = B(p, w)$ and the assumption that the behavior of the consumer is "a choice from a set".

This claim should not be interpreted as implying that "uniform inflation does not matter". We assumed, rather than concluded, that choice is made from a set independently of the way that the choice set is framed. Our model of choice is static and the consumer is assumed not to be affected in one decision from his choice in a previous decision. Inflation will affect behavior in a model where this strong assumption is relaxed.

Claim (Walras's Law):

If the preferences are monotonic, then any solution x to the consumer problem $B(p, w)$ is located on its budget curve (and, thus, $px(p, w) = w$).

Proof:

If not, then $px < w$. There is an $\varepsilon > 0$ such that $p(x_1 + \varepsilon, \ldots, x_K + \varepsilon) < w$. By monotonicity, $(x_1 + \varepsilon, \ldots, x_K + \varepsilon) \succ x$, thus contradicting the assumption that x is optimal in $B(p, w)$.

Claim:

If $\succsim$ is a continuous preference, then the demand function is continuous in prices (and also in w; see problem set).

Proof:

Once again, we could use the fact that the preferences have a continuous utility representation and apply a standard "maximum theorem". (Let $f(x)$ be a continuous function over X. Let A be a subset of some Euclidean space and B a function that attaches to every a in

A a compact subset of X such that its graph, $\{(a, x) \mid x \in B(a)\}$, is closed. Then the graph of the correspondence h from A into X, defined by $h(a) = \{x \in B(a) \mid f(x) \geq f(y) \text{ for all } y \in X\}$, is closed.) However, I prefer to present another proof, that does not use the notion of a utility function:

Assume not. Then, there is a sequence of price vectors p^n converging to p^* such that $x(p^*, w) = x^*$, and $x(p^n, w)$ does not converge to x^*. Thus, we can assume that (p^n) is a sequence converging to p^* such that for all n the distance $d(x(p^n, w), x^*) > \varepsilon$ for some positive ε.

All numbers p_k^n are greater than some positive number m. Therefore, all vectors $x(p^n, w)$ belong to some compact set (the hypercube of bundles with no quantity above w/m), and thus, without loss of generality (choosing a subsequence if necessary), we can assume that $x(p^n, w) \to y^*$ for some $y^* \neq x^*$.

Since $p^n x(p^n, w) \leq w$ for all n, it must be that $p^* y^* \leq w$, that is, $y^* \in B(p^*, w)$. Since x^* is the unique solution for $B(p^*, w)$, we have $x^* \succ y^*$. By the continuity of the preferences, there are neighborhoods B_{x^*} and B_{y^*} of x^* and y^* in which the strict preference is preserved. For sufficiently large n, $x(p^n, w)$ is in B_{y^*}. Choose a bundle z^* in the neighborhood B_{x^*} so that $p^* z^* < w$. For all sufficiently large n, $p^n z^* < w$; however, $z^* \succ x(p^n, w)$, which is a contradiction.

Comment:

The above proposition applies to the case in which for every budget set there is a unique bundle maximizing the consumer's preferences. The maximum theorem applied to the case in which some budget set has more than one maximizer states: if $\succsim$ is a continuous preference, then the set $\{(x, p, w) \mid x \succsim y \text{ for every } y \in B(p, w)\}$ is closed.

Rationalizable Demand Functions

As in the general discussion of choice, we will now examine whether choice procedures are consistent with the rational man model. We can think of various possible definitions of rationalization.

One approach is to look for a preference relation (without imposing any restrictions that fit the context of the consumer) such that the chosen element from any budget set is the unique bundle maximizing the preference relation in that budget set. Thus, we say that the preferences $\succsim$ *fully rationalize* the demand function x if for any (p, w) the bundle $x(p, w)$ is the unique $\succsim$ maximal bundle within $B(p, w)$.

Alternatively, we could say that "being rationalizable" means that there are preferences such that the consumer's behavior is consistent with maximizing those preferences, that is, for any (p, w) the bundle $x(p, w)$ is a $\succsim$ maximal bundle (not necessarily unique) within $B(p, w)$. This definition is "empty" since any demand function is consistent with maximizing the "total indifference" preference. This is why we usually say that the preferences $\succsim$ *rationalize* the demand function x if they are *monotonic*, and for any (p, w), the bundle $x(p, w)$ is a $\succsim$ maximal bundle within $B(p, w)$.

Of course, if behavior satisfies homogeneity of degree zero and Walras's law, it is still not necessarily rationalizable in any of those senses:

Example 1:

Consider the demand function of a consumer who spends all his wealth on the "more expensive" good:

$$x((p_1, p_2), w) = \begin{cases} (0, w/p_2) & if \quad p_2 \geq p_1 \\ (w/p_1, 0) & if \quad p_2 < p_1 \end{cases}.$$

This demand function is not entirely inconceivable, and yet it is not rationalizable. To see this, assume that it is fully rationalizable or rationalizable by $\succsim$. Consider the two budget sets $B((1, 2), 1)$ and $B((2, 1), 1)$. Since $x((1, 2), 1) = (0, 1/2)$ and $(1/2, 0)$ is an internal bundle in $B((1, 2), 1)$, by any of the two definitions of rationalizability it must be that $(0, 1/2) \succ (1/2, 0)$. Similarly, $x((2, 1), 1) = (1/2, 0)$ and $(0, 1/2)$ is an internal bundle in $B((2, 1), 1)$. Thus, $(0, 1/2) \prec (1/2, 0)$, a contradiction.

Example 2:

A consumer chooses a bundle $(z, z, \ldots, z)$, where z satisfies $z \Sigma p_k = w$.

This behavior is fully rationalized by any preferences according to which the consumer strictly prefers any bundle on the main diagonal over any bundle that is not (because, for example, he cares primarily about purchasing equal quantities from all sellers of the K goods), while on the main diagonal his preferences are according to "the more the better". These preferences rationalize his behavior in the first sense but are not monotonic.

This demand function is also fully rationalized by the monotonic preferences represented by the utility function $u(x_1, \ldots, x_K) = min\{x_1, \ldots, x_K\}$.

Example 3:

Consider a consumer who spends α_k of his wealth on commodity k (where $\alpha_k \geq 0$ and $\Sigma_{k=1}^{K}\alpha_k = 1$). This rule of behavior is not formulated as a maximization of some preference relation. It can however be fully rationalized by the preference relation represented by the Cobb-Douglas utility function $u(x) = \Pi_{k=1}^{K}x_k^{\alpha_k}$, a differentiable function with strictly positive derivatives in all interior points. A solution x^* to the consumer problem $B(p, w)$ must satisfy $x_k^* > 0$ for all k (notice that $u(x) = 0$ when $x_k = 0$ for some k). Given the differentiability of the preferences, a necessary condition for the optimality of x^* is that $v_k(x^*)/p_k = v_l(x^*)/p_l$ for all k and l where $v_k(x^*) = du/dx_k(x^*) = \alpha_k u(x^*)/x_k^*$ for all k. It follows that $p_k x_k^*/p_l x_l^* = \alpha_k/\alpha_l$ for all k and l and thus $x_k^* = \alpha_k w/p_k$ for all k.

Example 4:

Let $K = 2$. Consider the behavior of a consumer who allocates his wealth between commodities 1 and 2 in the proportion p_2/p_1 (the cheaper the good, the higher the share of the wealth devoted to it). Thus, $x_1 p_1/x_2 p_2 = p_2/p_1$ and $x_i(p, w) = (p_j/(p_i + p_j))w/p_i$. This demand function satisfies Walras's law as well as homogeneity of degree zero.

To see that this demand function is fully rationalizable, note that $x_i/x_j = p_j^2/p_i^2$ (for all i and j) and thus $p_1/p_2 = \sqrt{x_2}/\sqrt{x_1}$. The quasi-concave function $\sqrt{x_1} + \sqrt{x_2}$ satisfies the condition that the ratio of its partial derivatives is equal to $\sqrt{x_2}/\sqrt{x_1}$. Thus, for any (p, w), the bundle $x(p, w)$ is the solution to the maximization of $\sqrt{x_1} + \sqrt{x_2}$ in $B(p, w)$.

The Weak and Strong Axioms of Revealed Preferences

We now look for general conditions that will guarantee that a demand function $x(p, w)$ can be fully rationalized. A similar discussion could apply to another (probably more common in the textbooks) definition of rationalizability that requires that the bundle $x(p, w)$ maximizes a monotonic preference relation over $B(p, w)$. Of course, as we have seen, one does not necessarily need these general conditions to determine whether a particular demand function is rationalizable. Guessing is often an excellent strategy.

In the general discussion of choice functions, we saw that condition α was necessary and sufficient for a choice function to be derived from some preference relation. In the proof, we constructed a preference

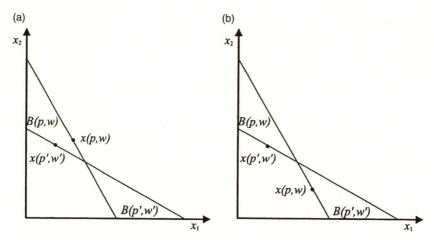

Figure 5.2
(a) Satisfies the weak axiom. (b) Does not satisfy the weak axiom.

relation out of the choices of the decision maker from sets containing two elements. However, in the context of a consumer, finite sets are not within the scope of the choice function.

As in Lecture 3 we will use the concept of "revealed preferences". Define $x \succ y$ if there is (p, w) so that both x and y are in $B(p, w)$ and $x = x(p, w)$. In such a case we will say that x is *revealed to be better* than y. As in Lecture 3 we will say that a preference relation $\succsim$ satisfies the *Weak Axiom of Revealed Preferences* if it is impossible that x is revealed to be better than y and y is revealed to be better than x. In the context of the consumer model, the Weak Axiom can be written as: if $x(p, w) \neq x(p', w')$ and $px(p', w') \leq w$, then $p'x(p, w) > w'$.

The Weak Axiom says that the defined binary relation $\succ$ is asymmetric. However, the relation is not necessarily complete: there can be two bundles x and y such that for any $B(p, w)$ containing both bundles, $x(p, w)$ is neither x nor y. Furthermore, in the general discussion, we guaranteed transitivity by looking at the union of a set in which a was revealed to be better than b and a set in which b was revealed to be as good as c. However, when the sets are budget sets, their union is not necessarily a budget set. (See fig. 5.2.)

Apparently the Weak Axiom is not a sufficient condition for extending the binary relation $\succ$, as defined above, into a complete and transitive relation (an example with three goods from Hicks (1956) is discussed in Mas-Colell et al. (1995)). A necessary and sufficient condition for a demand function x satisfying Walras's law and homogeneity of degree zero to be rationalized is the following:

Strong Axiom of Revealed Preference:

The Strong Axiom is a property of the demand function, which states that the relation $\succ$, derived from the demand function as before, is acyclical. This leaves open the question of whether $\succ$ can be extended into preferences. (Note that its transitive closure still may not be a complete relation.) The fact that it is possible to extend the relation $\succ$ into a full-fledged preference relation is a well-known result in Set Theory. In any case, the Strong Axiom is somewhat cumbersome, and using it to determine whether a certain demand function is rationalizable may not be a trivial task.

Comment:

The more standard definition of rationalizability requires finding monotonic preferences $\succsim$ such that for any (p, w), $x(p, w) \succsim y$ for all $y \in B(p, w)$. Proceeding to elicit preferences from the demand function, we infer from the existence of a budget set $B(p, w)$ for which $x = x(p, w)$ and $y \in B(p, w)$ only that x is weakly preferred to y. If, however, also $py < w$, we infer further that x is strongly preferred to y.

Decreasing Demand

A theoretical model is usually evaluated by the reasonableness of its implications. If we find that a model yields an absurd conclusion, we reconsider its assumptions. However, we should also be alert when we find that a model fails to yield highly intuitive properties, indicating that we may have assumed "too little".

In the context of the consumer model, we might wonder whether the intuition that demand for a good falls when its price increases is valid. We shall now see that the standard assumptions of rational consumer behavior do not guarantee that demand is decreasing. The following is an example of a preference relation that induces demand that is nondecreasing in the price of one of the commodities.

An Example in Which Demand for a Good May Increase with Price

Consider the preferences represented by the following utility function:

$$u(x_1, x_2) = \begin{cases} x_1 + x_2 & if \quad x_1 + x_2 < 1 \\ x_1 + 4x_2 & if \quad x_1 + x_2 \geq 1 \end{cases}.$$

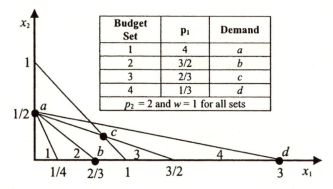

Figure 5.3
An example in which demand increases with price.

These preferences might reflect reasoning of the following type: "In the bundle x there are $x_1 + x_2$ units of vitamin A and $x_1 + 4x_2$ units of vitamin B. My first priority is to get enough vitamin A. However, once I satisfy my need for 1 unit of vitamin A, I move on to my second priority, which is to consume as much as possible of vitamin B". (See fig 5.3.)

Consider $x((p_1, 2), 1)$. Changing p_1 is like rotating the budget lines around the pivot bundle $(0, 1/2)$. At a high price p_1 (as long as $p_1 > 2$), the consumer demands $(0, 1/2)$. If the price is reduced to within the range $2 > p_1 > 1$, the consumer chooses the bundle $(1/p_1, 0)$. So far, the demand for the first commodity indeed increased when its price fell. However, in the range $1 > p_1 > 1/2$ we encounter an anomaly: the consumer buys as much as possible from the second good subject to the "constraint" that the sum of the goods is at least 1, that is, $x((p_1, 2), 1) = (1/(2 - p_1), (1 - p_1)/(2 - p_1))$.

The above preference relation is monotonic but not continuous. However, we can construct a close continuous preference that leads to demand that is increasing in p_1 in a similar domain. Let $\alpha_\delta(t)$ be a continuous and increasing function on $[1 - \delta, 1]$ where $\delta > 0$, so that $\alpha_\delta(t) = 0$ for all $t \le 1 - \delta$ and $\alpha_\delta(t) = 1$ for all $t \ge 1$. The utility function

$$u_\delta(x) = \alpha_\delta(x_1 + x_2)(x_1 + 4x_2) + (1 - \alpha_\delta(x_1 + x_2))(x_1 + x_2)$$

is continuous and monotonic. For δ close to 0, the function $u_\delta = u$ except in a narrow area below the set of bundles for which $x_1 + x_2 = 1$.

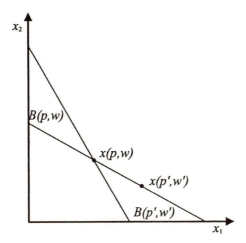

Figure 5.4
A compensated price change from (p, w) to (p', w').

Now, when $p_1 = 2/3$, the demand for the first commodity is $3/4$, whereas when $p_1 = 1$, the demand is at least $1 - 2\delta$. Thus, for a small enough δ the increase in p_1 involves an increase in the demand.

"The Law of Demand"

We are interested in comparing demand in different environments. We have just seen that the classic assumptions about the consumer do not allow us to draw a clear conclusion regarding the relation between a consumer's demand when facing $B(p, w)$ and his demand when facing $B(p + (0, \ldots, \varepsilon, \ldots, 0), w)$.

A clear conclusion can be drawn when we compare the consumer's demand when he faces the budget set $B(p, w)$ to his demand when facing $B(p', x(p, w)p')$. In this comparison we imagine the price vector changing from p to an arbitrary p' and wealth changing in such a way that the consumer has exactly the resources allowing him to consume the same bundle he consumed at (p, w). (See fig. 5.4.) It follows from the following claim that the compensated demand function $y(p') = x(p', p'x(p, w))$ satisfies the law of demand, that is, y_k is decreasing in p_k.

Claim:
Let x be a demand function satisfying Walras's law and WA. If $w' = p'x(p, w)$, then either $x(p', w') = x(p, w)$ or $[p' - p][x(p', w') - x(p, w)] < 0$.

Proof:

Assume that $x(p', w') \neq x(p, w)$. By Walras's law and the assumption that $w' = p'x(p, w)$:

$$[p' - p][x(p', w') - x(p, w)]$$
$$= p'x(p', w') - p'x(p, w) - px(p', w') + px(p, w)$$
$$= w' - w' - px(p', w') + w = w - px(p', w')$$

By WA the right-hand side of the equation is less than 0.

Bibliographic Notes

Recommended readings. Kreps 1990, 37–45; Mas-Colell et al. 1995, chapters 2, A–D; 3, D, J.

The material in this lecture, up to the discussion of differentiability, is fairly standard and closely parallels that found in Arrow and Hahn (1971) and Varian (1984).

Problem Set 5

Problem 1. (*Easy*)
Verify that when preferences are continuous, the demand function $x(p, w)$ is continuous in prices and in wealth (and not only in p).

Problem 2. (*Easy*)
Show that if a consumer has a homothetic preference relation, then his demand function is homogeneous of degree one in w.

Problem 3. (*Easy*)
Consider a consumer in a world with $K = 2$, who has a preference relation that is convex and quasi-linear in the first commodity. How does the demand for the first commodity change with w?

Problem 4. (*Moderately Difficult*)
Let $\succsim$ be a continuous preference relation (not necessarily strictly convex) and w a number. Consider the set $G = \{(p, x) \in \mathbb{R}^K \times \mathbb{R}^K |\ x \text{ is optimal in } B(p, w)\}$. (For some price vectors there could be more than one $(p, x) \in G$.) Calculate G for the case of $K = 2$ and preferences represented by $x_1 + x_2$. Show that, for any preference relation, G is a closed set.

Problem 5. (*Moderately difficult*)
Determine whether the following consumer behavior patterns are fully rationalized (assume $K = 2$):

  a. The consumer's demand function is $x(p, w) = (2w/(2p_1 + p_2), w/(2p_1 + p_2))$.
  b. The consumer consumes up to the quantity 1 of commodity 1 and spends his excess wealth on commodity 2.
  c. The consumer chooses the bundle (x_1, x_2) which satisfies $x_1/x_2 = p_1/p_2$ and costs w. (Does the utility function $u(x) = x_1^2 + x_2^2$ rationalize the consumer's behavior?)

Problem 6. (*Moderately difficult*)
In this question, we consider a consumer who behaves differently from the classic consumer we talked about in the lecture. Once again we consider a world with K commodities. The consumer's choice will be from budget sets. The consumer has in mind a preference relation that satisfies continuity,

monotonicity, and strict convexity; for simplicity, assume it is represented by a utility function u.

The consumer maximizes utility up to utility level u^0. If the budget set allows him to obtain this level of utility, he chooses the bundle in the budget set with the highest quantity of commodity 1 subject to the constraint that his utility is at least u^0.

a. Formulate the consumer's problem.
b. Show that the consumer's procedure yields a unique bundle.
c. Is this demand procedure rationalizable?
d. Does the demand function satisfy Walras's law?
e. Show that in the domain of (p, w) for which there is a feasible bundle yielding utility of at least u^0 the consumer's demand function for commodity 1 is decreasing in p_1 and increasing in w.
f. Is the demand function continuous?

Problem 7. (*Moderately difficult*)

It's a common practice in economics to view aggregate demand as being derived from the behavior of a "representative consumer". Give two examples of "well-behaved" consumer preference relations that can induce average behavior that is not consistent with maximization by a "representative consumer". (That is, construct two "consumers", 1 and 2, who choose the bundles x^1 and x^2 out of the budget set A and the bundles y^1 and y^2 out of the budget set B so that the choice of the bundle $(x^1 + x^2)/2$ from A and of the bundle $(y^1 + y^2)/2$ from B is inconsistent with the model of the rational consumer.)

Problem 8. (*Moderately difficult*)

A commodity k is *Giffen* if the demand for the $k'th$ good is increasing in p_k. A commodity k is *inferior* if the demand for the commodity decreases with wealth. Show that if there is a vector (p, w) such that the demand for the $k'th$ commodity is rising after its price has increased, then there is a vector (p', w') such that the demand of the $k'th$ commodity is falling after the income has increased (Giffen implies inferior).

Choice over Budget Sets and the Dual Consumer

Indirect Preferences

As an introduction to the first topic in this lecture, let us go back to the general choice function concept discussed in Lecture 3. Having in mind a preference relation $\succsim$ on a set X, the decision maker may want to construct a preference relation over the set D, the domain of his choice function. When assessing a choice problem in D, the decision maker may then ask himself which alternative he would choose if he had to choose from that set. The "rational" decision maker will prefer a set A over a set B if the alternative he intends to choose from A is preferable to that which he intends to choose from B. This leads us to the definition of $\succsim^*$, the *indirect preferences* induced from $\succsim$:

$$A \succsim^* B \text{ if } C_{\succsim}(A) \succsim C_{\succsim}(B).$$

The definition of indirect preferences ignores some considerations that might be taken into account when comparing choice sets. Excluded are considerations such as, "I prefer $A - \{b\}$ to A even though I intend to choose a in any case since I am afraid to make a mistake and choose b " or "I will choose a from A whether b is available or not, however, since I don't want to have to reject b, I prefer $A - \{b\}$ to A".

Of course, if u represents $\succsim$ and the choice function is well defined, $v(A) = u(C_{\succsim}(A))$ represents $\succsim^*$. We will refer to v as the *indirect utility function*.

Finally, note that sometimes (depending on the set D) one can reconstruct the choice function $C_{\succsim}(A)$ from the indirect preferences $\succsim^*$. For example, if $a \in A$ and $A \succ^* A - \{a\}$, then $C_{\succsim}(A) = a$.

The Consumer's Indirect Preferences

Let us return to the consumer who chooses bundles from budget sets. For simplicity, let us assume that the consumer holds the preference relation

$\succsim$ and $x(p, w)$ is always well-defined. The consumer might be interested in formulating indirect preferences when choosing a market to live in or when assessing the effect of tax reforms (affecting prices or wealth) on his welfare. Since a budget set is characterized by the $K + 1$ parameters (p, w), the above approach leads to the definition of the indirect preferences $\succsim^*$ on the set $\mathbb{R}_{++}^{K+1}$ as $(p, w) \succsim^* (p', w')$ if $x(p, w) \succsim x(p', w')$. Interpreting p in the standard manner, as prices prevailing in the market, defining indirect preferences in this way precludes considerations such as, "I prefer to live in an area where alcohol is very expensive even though I drink a lot".

The following are basic properties of the indirect preferences $\succsim^*$, induced from the preferences $\succsim$ on the bundle space. The first is an "invariance to presentation" property, which follows from the definition of indirect preferences independently of the properties of the consumer's preferences. The other three properties are: monotonicity (using the orders on the axis), continuity (using the topological structure), and "anti-convexity" (using the algebraic structure).

1. $(\lambda p, \lambda w) \sim^* (p, w)$ (this follows from $x(\lambda p, \lambda w) = x(p, w)$).
2. $\succsim^*$ is decreasing in p_k and strictly increasing in w (reducing the scope of the choice is never beneficial, and additional wealth makes it possible to consume bundles containing more of all commodities).
3. Let $\succsim$ be a continuous preference relation; then $x(p, w)$ is continuous. If $(p, w) \succ^* (p', w')$, then $y = x(p, w) \succ x(p', w') = y'$. By continuity there are balls B_y and $B_{y'}$ around y and y' accordingly such that for any $z \in B_y$ and $z' \in B_{y'}$ we have $z \succ z'$. By the continuity of the demand function there is a neighborhood around (p, w) such that the demand in this neighborhood is inside B_y, and there is a neighborhood around (p', w') such that the demand in this neighborhood is inside $B_{y'}$. For any two budget sets in these two neighborhoods $\succ^*$ is preserved.
4. If $(p^1, w^1) \succsim^* (p^2, w^2)$, then $(p^1, w^1) \succsim^* (\lambda p^1 + (1 - \lambda)p^2, \lambda w^1 + (1 - \lambda)w^2)$ for all $1 \geq \lambda \geq 0$. (See fig. 6.1.) (Thus, if v represents $\succsim^*$, then the preference relation is *quasi-convex*, that is, any set $\{(p, w)| v(p, w) \leq v(p^*, w^*)\}$ is convex.) To see this, let z be the best bundle in the budget set $B(\lambda p^1 + (1 - \lambda)p^2, \lambda w^1 + (1 - \lambda)w^2)$. Then $(\lambda p^1 + (1 - \lambda)p^2)z \leq \lambda w^1 + (1 - \lambda)w^2$ and therefore $p^1 z \leq w^1$ or $p^2 z \leq w^2$. Thus $z \in B(p^1, w^1)$ or $z \in B(p^2, w^2)$ and then $x(p^1, w^1) \succsim z$ or $x(p^2, w^2) \succsim z$. From $x(p^1, w^1) \succsim x(p^2, w^2)$ it follows that $x(p^1, w^1) \succsim z$.

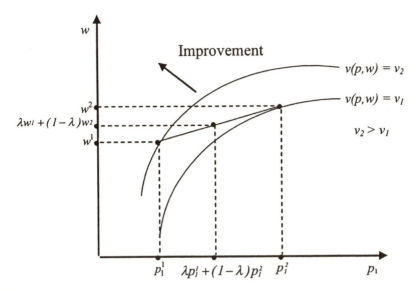

Figure 6.1
The indirect utility function is quasi-convex.

Example:

In the single commodity case, each $\succsim^*$-indifference curve is a ray. If we assume monotonicity of $\succsim$, the slope of an indifference curve through (p_1, w) is $x_1(p_1, w) = w/p_1$.

Roy's Identity

We will now look at a method of deriving the consumer demand function from indirect preferences. The idea is that starting from a budget set $B(p^*, w^*)$, any $B(p, w)$ for which $px(p^*, w^*) = w$ cannot be inferior to $B(p^*, w^*)$. The set of all (p, w) such that $px(p^*, w^*) = w$ is a tangent to the indifference curve of the indirect preferences through (p^*, w^*). Thus, knowing the indifference curve through (p^*, w^*), we can uncover the demand at (p^*, w^*).

Claim:

Assume that the demand function satisfies Walras's law. Let $H = \{(p, w)|(x(p^*, w^*), -1)(p, w) = 0\}$ for some (p^*, w^*). The hyperplane H is tangent to the $\succsim^*$-indifference curve through (p^*, w^*).

Proof:

Of course $(p^*, w^*) \in H$. For any $(p, w) \in H$, the bundle $x(p^*, w^*) \in B(p, w)$. Hence $x(p, w) \succsim x(p^*, w^*)$, and thus $(p, w) \succsim^* (p^*, w^*)$.

In the case in which $\succsim^*$ is represented by a differentiable function v, there is a unique tangent to the indifference curve through (p^*, w^*) characterized by:

$$T = \{(p, w) | \ (\partial v/\partial p_1(p^*, w^*), \ldots, \partial v/\partial p_K(p^*, w^*),$$
$$\partial v/\partial w(p^*, w^*))(p - p^*, w - w^*) = 0\}.$$

From the above claim and since $w^* = p^* x(p^*, w^*)$, we have also that

$$H = \{(p, w) | \ (x(p^*, w^*), -1)(p - p^*, w - w^*) = 0\}$$

is a tangent to the indifference curve through (p^*, w^*). Thus, $T = H$ and

$$(\partial v/\partial p_1(p^*, w^*), \ldots, \partial v/\partial p_K(p^*, w^*), \partial v/\partial w(p^*, w^*))$$

is proportional to the vector

$$(x_1(p^*, w^*), \ldots, x_K(p^*, w^*), -1).$$

Thus, we get the so called Roy identity:

$$-[\partial v/\partial p_k(p^*, w^*)]/[\partial v/\partial w(p^*, w^*)] = x_k(p^*, w^*).$$

The Dual Consumer

In the standard model, a consumer is equipped with a preference relation $\succsim$ and an initial bundle z. When facing the price vector p, he chooses to consume the $\succsim$-optimal bundle that can be obtained by exchanging the goods according to those prices. We refer to the problem of choosing a $\succsim$-best bundle in the set $\{x \mid px \leq pz\}$ as the *prime problem* and denote it by $P(p, z)$. Assuming that a solution to the problem exists and is unique, denote it by $x(p, z)$. The function x is the standard demand function.

Consider now another type of consumer. When holding a bundle z and facing the price vector p, he chooses the cheapest bundle that is as good as z. This behavior fits a context in which a consumer has a welfare target and seeks to reduce the costs involved in reaching it. We will refer to the problem $\min_x \{px \mid x \succsim z\}$ as the *dual problem* and denote it by $D(p, z)$. Assuming that a solution exists and is unique (which occurs, for example, when preferences are strictly convex and continuous), we denote the solution as $h(p, z)$, which is called the *Hicksian demand function*. The function $e(p, z) = ph(p, z)$ is called the *expenditure function*. Note the duality between the expenditure function and the consumer's indirect utility function.

Following are some properties of the Hicksian demand function and the expenditure function:

1. $h(p, z) = h(\lambda p, z)$. This follows from the fact that a bundle minimizes the function λpx in a set if and only if it minimizes the function px over that same set. Thus, $e(\lambda p, z) = \lambda e(p, z)$.

2. The Hicksian demand for the k'th commodity is decreasing in p_k. Note that $ph(p', z) \geq ph(p, z)$ for every p'. This is because $h(p', z) \succsim z$ and the bundle $h(p', z)$ is not less expensive than $h(p, z)$ for the price vector p. Thus, $(p' - p)(h(p', z) - h(p, z)) = (p'h(p', z) - p'h(p, z)) + (ph(p, z) - ph(p', z)) \leq 0$ and if $(p' - p) = (0, ..., \varepsilon, ..., 0)$ (with $\varepsilon > 0$), we obtain $h_k(p', z) - h_k(p, z) \leq 0$.
   In addition, $e(p, z)$ is increasing in p_k: if $p'_k \geq p_k$ for all k, then $e(p', z) = p'h(p', z) \geq ph(p', z) \geq ph(p, z) = e(p, z)$.

3. By continuity, $h(p, z) \sim z$. If $h(p, z) \succ z$, then there would be a cheaper bundle at least as good as z near $h(p, z)$.

4. By continuity $h(p, z)$ is continuous (verify!), as is $e(p, z)$.

5. The expenditure function is concave in p: let $x = h(\lambda p^1 + (1 - \lambda)p^2, z)$. By definition $x \succsim z$. Thus, $p^i x \geq p^i h(p^i, z)$ and $e(\lambda p^1 + (1 - \lambda)p^2, z) = (\lambda p^1 + (1 - \lambda)p^2)x \geq \lambda e(p^1, z) + (1 - \lambda)e(p^1, z)$.

6. (the Dual of Roy's identity) The hyperplane $H = \{(p, e) \mid e = ph(p^*, z)\}$ is tangent to the graph of the expenditure function at p^*. This follows from: (i) $(p^*, e(p^*, z))$ is in H and (ii) $ph(p^*, z) \geq ph(p, z)$ for all p^*.

Duality

In daily discourse we consider the following two statements to be equivalent:

1. The maximal distance a turtle can travel in 1 day is 1 km.
2. The minimal time it takes a turtle to travel 1 km is 1 day.

This equivalence in fact relies on two "hidden" assumptions:

a. For (1) to imply (2), we need to assume that the turtle travels a positive distance in any period of time. Contrast this with the case in which the turtle's speed is 2 km/day, but after half a day it must rest for half a day. In this case, the maximal distance it can travel in 1 day is 1 km, but it can travel this distance in only half a day.

b. For (2) to imply (1), we need to assume that the turtle cannot "jump" a positive distance in zero time. Contrast this with the case in which the turtle's speed is 1 km/day, but after a day of traveling it can "jump" 1 km. Thus, it needs 1 day to travel 1 km, but within 1 day it can travel 2 km.

The assumptions that in any positive interval of time the turtle can travel a positive distance and that the turtle cannot "jump" are sufficient for the equivalence of (1) and (2). Let $M(t)$ be the maximal distance the turtle can travel in time t. Assume that the function M is strictly increasing and continuous. Then, the statement "The maximal distance a turtle can travel in t^* is x^*" is equivalent to the statement "The minimal time it takes a turtle to travel x^* is t^*".

If the maximal distance that the turtle can travel within t^* is x^* and if it covers the distance x^* in $t < t^*$, then by the strict monotonicity of M the turtle could cover a distance larger than x^* in t^*, a contradiction.

If it takes t^* for the turtle to cover the distance x^* and if it travels the distance $x > x^*$ in t^*, then by the continuity of M at some $t < t^*$ the turtle will already be beyond the distance x^*, a contradiction.

With this intuition in mind, we return to the world of the consumer. Given preferences satisfying monotonicity and continuity, a regular consumer who holds x^* is happy in the sense that he cannot exchange the bundle for a better one if and only if a dual consumer who holds x^* is happy, in the sense that there is no cheaper bundle as good as x^*.

Claim:

A bundle x^* is a solution to the problem $P(p, x^*)$ if and only if it is a solution to the dual problem $D(p, x^*)$.

Proof:

1. If x^* is not a solution to $D(p, x^*)$, then there exists a strictly cheaper bundle x for which $x \succsim x^*$. For some positive vector ε (i.e., $\varepsilon_k > 0$ for all k), it still holds that $p(x + \varepsilon) < px^*$. By monotonicity $x + \varepsilon \succ x \succsim x^*$, contradicting the assumption that x^* is a solution to $P(p, x^*)$.

2. If x^* is not a solution to the problem $P(p, x^*)$, then there exists an x such that $px \leq px^*$ and $x \succ x^*$. By continuity, for some nonnegative vector $\varepsilon \neq 0$, $x - \varepsilon$ is a bundle such that $x - \varepsilon \succ x^*$ and

$p(x - \varepsilon) < px^*$, contradicting the assumption that x^* is a solution to $D(p, x^*)$.

Bibliographic Notes

Recommended readings. Kreps 1990, 45–63; Mas-Colell et al. 1995, chapters 2, E–F; 3, D–G, I–J.

Roy and Hicks are the sources for most of the material in this lecture. Specifically, the concept of the indirect utility function is due to Roy (1942); the concept of the expenditure function is due to Hicks (1946); and the concepts of consumer surplus used in problem 6 are due to Hicks (1939). See also McKenzie (1957). For a full representation of the duality idea, see, for example, Varian (1984) and Diewert (1982).

Problem Set 6

Problem 1. (*Easy*)
In a world with two commodities, consider a consumer's preferences that are represented by the utility function $u(x_1, x_2) = min\{x_1, x_2\}$.

  a. Calculate the consumer's demand function.
  b. Verify that the preferences satisfy convexity.
  c. Calculate the indirect utility function $v(p, w)$.
  d. Verify Roy's identity.
  e. Calculate the expenditure function $e(p, u)$ and verify the dual Roy's identity.

Problem 2. (*Standard*)
Imagine that you are reading a paper in which the author uses the indirect utility function $v(p_1, p_2, w) = w/p_1 + w/p_2$. You suspect that the author's conclusions in the paper are the outcome of the "fact" that the function v is inconsistent with the model of the rational consumer. Take the following steps to make sure that this is not the case:

  a. Use Roy's identity to derive the demand function.
  b. Show that if demand is derived from a smooth utility function, then the indifference curve at the point (x_1, x_2) has the slope $-\sqrt{x_2}/\sqrt{x_1}$.
  c. Construct a utility function with the property that the ratio of the partial derivatives at the bundle (x_1, x_2) is $\sqrt{x_2}/\sqrt{x_1}$.
  d. Calculate the indirect utility function derived from this utility function. Do you arrive at the original $v(p_1, p_2, w)$? If not, can the original indirect utility function still be derived from another utility function satisfying the property in (c)?

Problem 3. (*Standard*)
A consumer with wealth w is interested in purchasing only one unit of one of the items included in a (finite) set A. All items are *indivisible*. The consumer does not derive any "utility" from leftover wealth. The consumer evaluates commodity $x \in A$ by the number V_x (where the value of not purchasing any of the goods is 0). The price of commodity $x \in A$ is $p_x > 0$.

  a. Formulate the consumer problem.
  b. Check the properties of the indirect preferences (homogeneity of degree zero, mono- tonicity, continuity, and quasi-convexity).

c. Calculate an indirect utility function for the case in which $A = \{a, b\}$ and $V_a > V_b > 0$.

Problem 4. (*Moderate*)
Assume that the consumer's preferences $\succsim$ satisfy monotonicity, continuity, and strict convexity. Show that the bundle x is the best element in $B(p, w)$ if and only if for all $y \in B(p, w)$ different from x, there exists a budget set $B(p', w')$ containing y and not x such that $(p, w) \succ^* (p', w')$.

Problem 5. (*Moderately difficult*)
Show that if the preferences are monotonic, continuous, and strictly convex, then the Hicksian demand function $h(p, z)$ is continuous.

Problem 6. (*Moderately difficult*)
One way to compare budget sets is by using the indirect preferences that involve comparing $x(p, w)$ and $x(p', w)$.

Following are two other approaches to making such a comparison.
Define:

$$CV(p, p', w) = w - e(p', z) = e(p, z) - e(p', z)$$

where $z = x(p, w)$.

This is the answer to the question: What is the change in wealth that would be equivalent, from the perspective of (p, w), to the change in price vector from p to p'?
Define:

$$EV(p, p', w) = e(p, z') - w = e(p, z') - e(p', z')$$

where $z' = x(p', w)$.

This is the answer to the question: What is the change in wealth that would be equivalent, from the perspective of (p', w), to the change in price vector from p to p'?

Now, solve the following exercises regarding a consumer in a two-commodity world with a utility function u:

a. For the case of preferences represented by $u(x_1, x_2) = x_1 + x_2$, calculate the two *consumer surplus* measures.
b. Assume that the first good is a normal good (the demand is increasing with wealth). What is the relation of the two measures to the "area below the demand function" (which is a standard third definition of consumer surplus)?
c. Explain why the two measures are identical if the individual has quasilinear preferences in the second commodity and in a domain where the two commodities are consumed in positive quantities.

Problem 7. (*Moderately difficult*)

a. Verify that you know the envelope theorem, which states conditions under which the following is correct: consider a maximization problem $\max_x \{u(x, \alpha_1, \ldots, \alpha_n) \mid g(x, \alpha_1, \ldots, \alpha_n) = 0\}$. Let $V(\alpha_1, \ldots, \alpha_n)$ be the value of the maximization.

Then, $\frac{\partial V}{\partial \alpha_i}(a_1, \ldots, a_n) = \frac{\partial(u - \lambda g)}{\partial \alpha_i}(x^*(a_1, \ldots, \alpha_n), a_1, \ldots, \alpha_n)$ where $x^*(a_1, \ldots, \alpha_n)$ is the solution to the maximization problem, and λ is the Lagrange multiplier associated with the solution of the maximization problem.

b. Derive the Roy's identity from the envelope theorem (hint: show that in this context $\frac{\partial V / \partial \alpha_i}{\partial V / \partial \alpha_j}(a_1, \ldots, a_n) = \frac{\partial g / \partial \alpha_i}{\partial g / \partial \alpha_j}(x^*(a_1, \ldots, \alpha_n), a_1, \ldots, \alpha_n))$.

c. What makes it is easy to prove Roy's identity without using the envelope theorem?

The Producer

The Producer

We now turn to a brief discussion of the basic concepts of producer theory. Since only a few new modeling ideas are involved, we make do with a short introduction to the basic concepts.

We think about a producer as an economic agent who has the ability to transform one vector of commodities into another.

Technology

Let $1, \ldots, K$ be commodities. A vector z in $\mathbb{R}^K$ is interpreted as a production combination; positive components in z are outputs, and negative components are inputs.

A producer's choice set is called a *technology* and specifies the production constraints.

The following restrictions are usually placed on the technology space (fig. 7.1):

1. $0 \in Z$ (this is interpreted to mean that the producer can remain "idle").
2. There is no $z \in Z \cap \mathbb{R}_+^K$ besides the vector 0 (no production with no resources).
3. *Free disposal*: If $z \in Z$ and $z' \leq z$, then $z' \in Z$ (nothing prevents the producer from being inefficient in the sense that he uses more resources than necessary to produce the same amount of commodities).
4. Z is a closed set.
5. Z is a convex set. (This assumption embodies decreasing marginal productivity. Together with the assumption that $0 \in Z$, it implies *nonincreasing returns to scale*: if $z \in Z$, then for all $\lambda < 1$, $\lambda z \in Z$.)

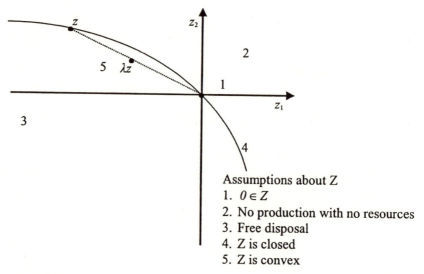

Assumptions about Z
1. $0 \in Z$
2. No production with no resources
3. Free disposal
4. Z is closed
5. Z is convex

Figure 7.1
Technology.

The Production Function

Consider the case in which commodity K is produced from commodities $1, \ldots, K-1$, that is, for all $z \in Z$, $z_K \geq 0$ and for all $k \neq K$, $z_k \leq 0$. In this case, another way of specifying the technological constraints on the producer is by a *production function* that specifies, for any positive vector of inputs $v \in \mathbb{R}_+^{K-1}$, the maximum amount of commodity K that can be produced.

If we start from technology Z, we can derive the production function by defining

$$f(v) = max\{x| \ (-v, x) \in Z\}.$$

Alternatively, if we start from the production function f, we can derive the " technology" by defining $Z(f) = \{(-w, x)| \ x \leq y \text{ and } w \geq v \text{ for some } y = f(v)\}.$ If the function f satisfies the assumptions of $f(0) = 0$, increasing, continuity, and concavity, then $Z(f)$ satisfies the above assumptions.

The Producer's Preferences

We think of the producer as an agent who chooses a point z in his technology Z and cares about the outcome vector (z, π) where π are his profits. For any given price vector p, the producer faces choice sets of the type $B(p) = \{(z, \pi)| \ z \in Z \text{ and } \pi = pz\}$. Essentially, the producer's preferences are modeled just as any other preference relation over the (z, π) space. With this formalization in mind, it is clear that the standard assumption according to which the producer cares about profits is a very special case.

For concreteness, let us focus on a producer who is able to produce a single commodity (with its quantity denoted by y) using K inputs. Denote a vector of input quantities by $a = (a_1, \ldots, a_K)$. Let $y = f(a_1, \ldots, a_K)$ be the producer's production function. A rational producer maximizes a preference relation over all tuples $(a_1, \ldots, a_K, y, \pi)$ under the constraint $y = f(a)$ and $\pi = p_y y - p_a a$ where p_y is the price of the production good and p_a is a vector of input prices. It is worth mentioning several reasonable alternative targets, each of which could serve as the starting point of an alternative producer theory:

1. The producer maximizes production y given the constraint $\pi \geq 0$.
2. The producer is committed to produce at least y^* units of production and maximizes profits given the constraint $y \geq y^*$.
3. The producer maximizes the ratio between profits and costs. That is, his maximization problem is: $\max \frac{\pi}{p_a a}$, which is equivalent to $\max \frac{\pi}{p_y f(a)}$.
4. The producer already employs a_1^* workers and will incur a cost c for each worker he fires. Thus, he maximizes: $\pi - c \max\{0, a_1^* - a_1\}$.
5. The producer divides his profits equally among the workers and seeks to maximize the amount each of them receives: $max[\pi/a_1]$.
6. The producer maximizes a preference relation over $(a_1, \ldots, a_K, y)$ and ignores profits.
7. The producer has a preference relation that balances between π and the amount of pollution he creates (which is a function of inputs).
8. The producer knows that there exists an inelastic demand M for his product. If he produces y, his competitor will produce $M - y$, and his profits will be $\pi' = p_y(M - y) - \min_{f(a) = M - y} p_a a$. The producer seeks to maximize $\pi - \pi'$.
9. The producer maximizes his profits, π...

The rest of the chapter presents a very basic analysis of the profit-maximizing producer's problem.

The Supply Function of the Profit Maximizing Producer

We will now discuss the producer's behavior. The producer's problem is defined as $max_{z \in Z} pz$.

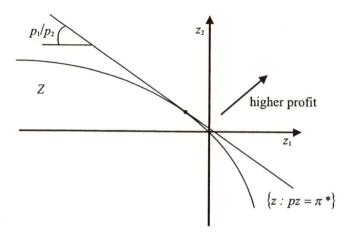

Figure 7.2
Profit maximization.

The existence of a unique solution for the producer's problem requires some additional assumptions such as that Z be *bounded from above* (i.e., there is some bound B such that $B \geq z_k$ for any $z \in Z$) and that Z be *strictly convex* (i.e., if z and z' are in Z, then the combination $\lambda z + (1 - \lambda)z'$ is an internal point in Z for any $1 > \lambda > 0$).

When the producer's problem has a unique solution, we denote it by $z(p)$. We refer to the function $z(p)$ as the *supply function*. Note that it specifies both the producer's supply of outputs and its demand for inputs. Define the *profit function* by $\pi(p) = max_{z \in Z} pz$.

Recall that when discussing the consumer, we specified the preferences and we described his behavior as making a choice from a budget set that had been determined by prices. The consumer's behavior (demand) specified the dependence of his consumption on prices. In the case of the producer, we specify the technology and describe his behavior as maximizing a profit function that is determined by prices. The producer's behavior (supply) specifies the dependence of output and the consumption of inputs on prices.

In the case of the producer, preferences are linear and the constraint is a convex set, whereas in the consumer model the constraint is a linear inequality and preferences are convex. The structure (continuity and convexity) is imposed on the producer's choice set and on the consumer's preferences. Thus, the producer's problem is similar to the consumer's *dual* problem. (See fig. 7.2.)

Properties of the Supply and Profit Functions

Let us turn to some of the properties of the supply and profit functions. The properties and their proofs are analogous to the properties and proofs in the discussion of the consumer's dual problem.

Supply Function

1. $z(\lambda p) = z(p)$. (The producer's preferences are induced by the price vector p and are identical to those induced by the price vector λp.)
2. z is continuous.
3. Assume the supply function is well defined. If $z(p) \neq z(p')$, we have $(p - p')[z(p) - z(p')] = p[z(p) - z(p')] + p'[z(p') - z(p)] > 0$. In particular, if (only) the k'th price increases, z_k increases; that is, if k is an output ($z_k > 0$), the supply of k increases; and if k is an input ($z_k < 0$), the demand for k decreases. Note that this result, called *the law of supply*, applies to the standard supply function (unlike the law of demand, which was applied to the compensated demand function).

Profit Function

1. $\pi(\lambda p) = \lambda \pi(p)$. (Follows from $z(\lambda p) = z(p)$.)
2. π is continuous. (Follows from the continuity of the supply function.)
3. π is convex. (For all p, p' and λ, if z maximizes profits with $\lambda p + (1 - \lambda)p'$, then $\pi(\lambda p + (1 - \lambda)p') = \lambda pz + (1 - \lambda)p'z \leq \lambda\pi(p) + (1 - \lambda)\pi(p')$.)
4. *Hotelling's lemma*: For any vector p^*, $\pi(p) \geq pz(p^*)$ for all p. Therefore, the hyperplane $\{(p, \pi) \mid \pi = pz(p^*)\}$ is tangent to $\{(p, \pi) \mid \pi = \pi(p)\}$, the graph of function π at the point $(p^*, \pi(p^*))$. If π is differentiable, then $d\pi/dp_k(p^*) = z_k(p^*)$.
5. From Hotelling's lemma it follows that if π is twice continuously differentiable, then $dz_j/dp_k(p^*) = dz_k/dp_j(p^*)$.

The Cost Function

If we are interested in the firm's behavior only in the output market (but not in the input markets), it is sufficient to specify the costs associated with the production of any combination of outputs as opposed to the details of the production function. Thus, for a producer of the commodities $L + 1, \ldots, K$, we define $c(p, y)$ to be the minimal cost

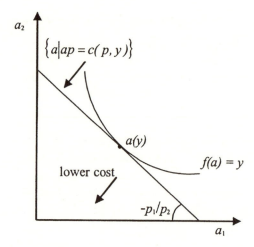

Figure 7.3
Cost Minimization.

associated with the production of the combination $y \in \mathbb{R}_+^{K-L}$ given the price vector $p \in \mathbb{R}_{++}^{L}$ of the input commodities $1, \ldots, L$. If the model's primitive is a technology Z, we have $c(p, y) = min_a\{pa|\ (-a, y) \in Z\}$. (See fig. 7.3.)

Discussion

In the conventional economic approach, we allow the consumer " general" preferences but restrict producer goals to profit maximization. Thus, a consumer who consumes commodities in order to destroy his health is within the scope of our discussion, whereas a producer who cares about the welfare of his workers or has in mind a target other than profit maximization is not. This is odd since there are various empirically plausible alternative targets for a producer. For example, it seems that the goal of some producers is to increase production subject to not incurring a loss. Some firms are managed so as to increase the managers' salaries with less regard for the level of profits.

I sometimes wonder why this difference exists between the generality of consumer preferences and the narrowness of the producer objectives. It might be that this is simply the result of mathematical convenience. I don't think this is a result of an ideological conspiracy. But, by making profit maximization the key assumption about producer behavior, do we not run the risk that students will interpret it to be the exclusive normative criterion guiding a firm's actions?

Bibliographic Notes

Recommended readings. Kreps 1990, chapter 8; Mas-Colell et al. 1995, chapter 5, A–D, G.

The material in this lecture (apart from the discussion) is standard and can be found in any microeconomics textbook. Debreu (1959) is an excellent source.

Problem Set 7

Problem 1. (*Easy*)
Assume that technology Z and the production function f describe the same producer who produces commodity K using inputs $1, \ldots, K - 1$. Show that Z is a convex set if and only if f is a concave function.

Problem 2. (*Boring*)
Here is a very standard exercise (if you have not done it in the past, it may be " fun" to do it " once in a lifetime"): calculate the supply function $z(p)$ for each of the following production functions:

   a. $f(a) = a_1^\alpha$ for $\alpha \leq 1$.
   b. $h(a) = min\{a_1, a_2\}$.

Problem 3. (*Easy*)
Consider a producer who uses L inputs to produce $K - L$ outputs. Denote by w the price vector of the L inputs. Let $a_k(w, y)$ be the demand for the k'th input when the price vector is w and the output vector he wishes to produce is y. Show the following:

   a. $C(\lambda w, y) = \lambda C(w, y)$.
   b. C is nondecreasing in any input price w_k.
   c. C is concave in w.
   d. Shepherd's lemma: If C is differentiable, $dC/dw_k(w, y) = a_k(w, y)$ (the k'th input commodity).
   e. If C is twice continuously differentiable, then for any two commodities j and k, $da_k/dw_j(w, y) = da_j/dw_k(w, y)$.

Problem 4. (*Moderately difficult. Based on Radner (1993).*)
It is usually assumed that the cost function C is convex in the output vector. Much of the research on production has been aimed at investigating conditions under which convexity is induced from more primitive assumptions about the production process. Convexity often fails when the product is related to the gathering of information or data processing.

   Consider, for example, a firm conducting a telephone survey immediately following a TV program. Its goal is to collect information about as many viewers as possible within 4 units of time. The wage paid to each worker is w (even when he is idle). In one unit of time, a worker can talk to one respondent or be involved in the transfer of information to or from exactly one colleague. At the end of the 4 units of time, the collected information must be in the hands of one colleague (who will announce the results). Define the firm's product, calculate the cost function, and examine its convexity.

Problem 5. (*Moderately difficult*)
Consider a firm producing one commodity using L inputs, which maximizes production subject to the constraint of nonnegative profits. Show that under reasonable assumptions, the firm's supply function satisfies Homogeneity of degree 0, monotonicity in prices, and continuity.

Problem 6. (*Standard*)
An event that could have occurred with probability 0.5 either did or did not occur. A firm must provide a report in the form of " the event occurred" or " the event did not occur". The quality of the report (the firm's product), denoted by q, is the probability that the report is correct. Each of k experts (input) prepares an independent recommendation that is correct with probability $1 > p > 0.5$. The firm bases its report on the k recommendations in order to maximize q.

   a. Calculate the production function $q = f(k)$ for (at least) $k = 1, 2, 3$.
   b. We say that a " discrete" production function is concave if the sequence of marginal product is nonincreasing. Is the firm's production function concave?

Assume that the firm will get a prize of M if its report is actually correct. Assume that the wage of each worker is w.

   c. Explain why it is true that if f is concave, the firm chooses k^* so that the k^*th worker is the last one for whom marginal revenue exceeds the cost of a single worker.
   d. Is this conclusion true in our case?

Problem 7. (*Moderately difficult*)
Come up with a theory for the producer who maximizes production given the constraint of achieving a level of profit ρ (and does not produce at all if he cannot).

   a. Show conditions under which the producer's problem has a unique solution for every price vector.
   b. How does the supply of the good change with its price and the price of any of the input goods?.
   c. What can you say about the change in producer behavior as ρ increases (in the range where he does indeed produce)?
   d. Are there any other observations you can think of (and prove ...)?

Expected Utility

Lotteries

When thinking about decision making, we often distinguish between actions and consequences. An action is chosen and leads to a consequence. The rational man has preferences over the set of consequences and is supposed to choose a feasible action that leads to the most desired consequence. In our discussion of the rational man, we have so far not distinguished between actions and consequences since it was unnecessary for modeling situations where each action deterministically leads to a particular consequence.

In this lecture we will discuss a decision maker in an environment in which the correspondence between actions and consequences is not deterministic but *stochastic*. The choice of an action is viewed as choosing a lottery where the prizes are the consequences. We will be interested in preferences and choices over the set of lotteries.

Let Z be a set of consequences (prizes). In this lecture we assume that Z is a finite set. A *lottery* is a probability measure on Z, that is, a lottery p is a function that assigns a nonnegative number $p(z)$ to each prize z, where $\Sigma_{z \in Z} p(z) = 1$. The number $p(z)$ is taken to be the objective probability of obtaining the prize z given the lottery p.

Denote by $[z]$ the degenerate lottery for which $[z](z) = 1$. We will use the notation $\alpha x \oplus (1 - \alpha)y$ to denote the lottery in which the prize x is realized with probability α and the prize y with probability $1 - \alpha$.

Denote by $L(Z)$ the (infinite) space containing all lotteries with prizes in Z. Given the set of consequences Z, the space of lotteries $L(Z)$ can be identified with a simplex in Euclidean space: $\{x \in \mathbb{R}_+^Z | \Sigma x_z = 1\}$ where $\mathbb{R}_+^Z$ is the set of functions from Z into $\mathbb{R}_+$. The extreme points of the simplex correspond to the degenerate lotteries, where one prize is received in probability 1. We will discuss preferences over $L(Z)$.

An implicit assumption in the above formalism is that the decision maker does not care about the nature of the random factors but only about the distribution of consequences. To appreciate this point, consider a case in which the probability of rain is $1/2$ and $Z = \{z_1, z_2\}$, where $z_1 =$ "having an umbrella" and $z_2 =$ "not having an umbrella". A "lottery" in which you have z_1 if it is raining and z_2 if it is not, should not be considered equivalent to the "lottery" in which you have z_1 if it is not raining and z_2 if it is. Thus, we have to be careful not to apply the model in contexts where the attitude toward the consequence depends on the event realized in each possible contingence.

Preferences

Let us think about examples of "sound" preferences over a space $L(Z)$. Following are some examples:

- *Preference for uniformity*: The decision maker prefers the lottery that is less disperse where dispersion is measured by $\Sigma_z(p(z) - 1/|Z|)^2$.
- *Preference for most likelihood*: The decision maker prefers p to q if $max_z p(z)$ is greater than $max_z q(z)$.
- *The size of the support*: The decision maker evaluates each lottery by the number of prizes that can be realized with positive probability, that is, by the size of the support of the lottery, $supp(p) = \{z | p(z) > 0\}$. He prefers a lottery p over a lottery q if $|supp(p)| \leq |supp(q)|$.

These three examples are degenerate in the sense that the preferences ignored the consequences and were dependent on the probability vectors alone. In the following examples, the preferences involve evaluation of the prizes as well.

- *Increasing the probability of a "good" outcome*: The set Z is partitioned into two disjoint sets G and B (good and bad), and between two lotteries the decision maker prefers the lottery p that yields "good" prizes with higher probability.
- *The worst case*: The decision maker evaluates lotteries by the *worst possible* case. He attaches a number $v(z)$ to each prize z and $p \succsim q$ if $min\{v(z) | p(z) > 0\} \geq min\{v(z) | q(z) > 0\}$. This criterion is often used in computer science, where one algorithm is preferred to another if it functions better in the worst case independently of the likelihood of the worst case occurring.
- *Comparing the most likely prize*: The decision maker considers the prize in each lottery that is most likely (breaking ties in some

arbitrary way) and compares two lotteries according to a basic preference relation over Z.

- *Lexicographic preferences*: The prizes are ordered $z_1, \ldots, z_K$, and the lottery p is preferred to q if $(p(z_1), \ldots, p(z_K)) \geq_L (q(z_1), \ldots, q(z_K))$.

- *Expected utility*: A number $v(z)$ is attached to each prize, and a lottery p is evaluated according to its expected v, that is, according to $\Sigma_z p(z) v(z)$. Thus,

$$p \succsim q \text{ if } U(p) = \Sigma_{z \in Z} p(z) v(z) \geq U(q) = \Sigma_{z \in Z} q(z) v(z).$$

Note that the above examples constitute ingredients that could be combined in various ways to form an even richer class of examples. For example, one preference can be employed as long as it is "decisive", and a second preference can be used to break ties when it is not.

The richness of examples calls for the classification of preference relations over lotteries and the study of properties that these relations satisfy. The methodology we follow is to formally state general principles (axioms) that may apply to preferences over the space of lotteries. Each axiom carries with it a consistency requirement or involves a procedural aspect of decision making. When a set of axioms characterizes a family of preferences, we will consider the set of axioms as justification for focusing on that specific family.

von Neumann and Morgenstern Axiomatization

The version of the von Neumann and Morgenstern axiomatization presented here uses two axioms, the independence and continuity axioms.

The Independence Axiom

In order to state the first axiom, we require an additional concept, called *Compound lotteries* (fig. 8.1): Given a K-tuple of lotteries $(p^k)_{k=1,\ldots,K}$ and a K-tuple of nonnegative numbers $(\alpha_k)_{k=1,\ldots,K}$ that sum up to 1, define $\oplus_{k=1}^{K} \alpha_k p^k$ to be the lottery for which $(\oplus_{k=1}^{K} \alpha_k p^k)(z) = \Sigma_{k=1}^{K} \alpha_k p^k(z)$. Verify that $\oplus_{k=1}^{K} \alpha_k p^k$ is indeed a lottery. When only two lotteries p^1 and p^2 are involved, we use the notation $\alpha_1 p^1 \oplus (1 - \alpha_1) p^2$.

We think of $\oplus_{k=1}^{K} \alpha_k p^k$ as a compound lottery with the following two stages:

Stage 1: It is randomly determined which of the lotteries $p^1, \ldots, p^K$ is realized; α_k is the probability that p^k is realized.

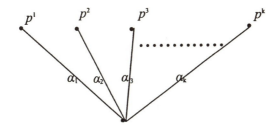

Figure 8.1
The compound lottery $\oplus_{k=1}^{K} \alpha_k p^k$.

Stage 2: The prize received is randomly drawn from the lottery determined in stage 1.

The random factors in the two stages are taken to be independent. When we compare two compound lotteries, $\alpha p \oplus (1 - \alpha) r$ and $\alpha q \oplus (1 - \alpha) r$, we tend to simplify the comparison and form our preference on the basis of the comparison between p and q. This intuition is translated into the following axiom:

Independence (I):
For any $p, q, r \in L(Z)$ and any $\alpha \in (0, 1)$,

$$p \succsim q \text{ iff } \alpha p \oplus (1 - \alpha) r \succsim \alpha q \oplus (1 - \alpha) r.$$

The following property follows from I:

I^*:
Let $\{p^k\}_{k=1,...,K}$, be a vector lotteries, q^{k^*} a lottery, and $(\alpha_k)_{k=1,...,K}$ an array of nonnegative numbers such that $\alpha_{k^*} > 0$ and $\sum_k \alpha_k = 1$. Then,

$$\oplus_{k=1}^{K} \alpha_k p^k \succsim \oplus_{k=1}^{K} \alpha_k q^k \text{ when } p^k = q^k \text{ for all } k \text{ but } k^* \text{ iff } p^{k^*} \succsim q^{k^*}.$$

To see it,

$$\oplus_{k=1,...,K} \alpha_k p^k = \alpha_{k^*} p^{k^*} \oplus (1 - \alpha_{k^*})(\oplus_{k \neq k^*} [\alpha_k / (1 - \alpha_{k^*})] p^k) \succsim$$

$$\alpha_{k^*} q^{k^*} \oplus (1 - \alpha_{k^*})(\oplus_{k \neq k^*} [\alpha_k / (1 - \alpha_{k^*})] p^k) = \oplus_{k=1}^{K} \alpha_k q^k \text{ iff } p^{k^*} \succsim q^{k^*}.$$

The Continuity Axiom
Once again we will employ a continuity assumption that is basically the same as the one we employed for the consumer model. Continuity means that the preferences are not overly sensitive to small changes in the probabilities.

Continuity (C):

If $p \succ q$, then there are neighborhoods $B(p)$ of p and $B(q)$ of q (when presented as vectors in $\mathbb{R}_+^{|Z|}$), such that

for all $p' \in B(p)$ and $q' \in B(q), p' \succ q'$.

Verify that the continuity assumption implies the following property, which sometimes is presented as an alternative definition of continuity:

C^*:

If $p \succ q \succ r$, then there exists $\alpha \in (0,1)$ such that

$$q \sim [\alpha p \oplus (1 - \alpha)r].$$

Let us check whether some of the examples we discussed earlier satisfy these two axioms.

- *Expected utility*: Note that the function $U(p)$ is linear:

$$U(\oplus_{k=1}^K \alpha_k p^k) = \sum_{z \in Z} [\oplus_{k=1}^K \alpha_k p^k](z)v(z) = \sum_{z \in Z} \left[\sum_{k=1}^K \alpha_k p^k(z) \right] v(z)$$

$$= \sum_{k=1}^K \alpha_k \left[\sum_{z \in Z} p^k(z)v(z) \right] = \sum_{k=1}^K \alpha_k U(p^k).$$

It follows that any such preference relation satisfies I. Since the function $U(p)$ is continuous in the probability vector, it also satisfies C.

- *Increasing the probability of a "good" consequence*: Such a preference relation satisfies the two axioms since it can be represented by the expectation of v where $v(z) = 1$ for $z \in G$ and $v(z) = 0$ for $z \in B$.

- *Preferences for most likelihood*: This preference relation is continuous (as the function $max\{p_1, \ldots, p_K\}$ that represents it is continuous in probabilities). It does not satisfy I since, for example, although $[z_1] \sim [z_2]$, $[z_1] = 1/2[z_1] \oplus 1/2[z_1] \succ 1/2[z_1] \oplus 1/2[z_2]$.

- *Lexicographic preferences*: Such a preference relation satisfies I but not C (verify).

- *The worst case*: The preference relation does not satisfy C. In the two-prize case where $v(z_1) > v(z_2)$, $[z_1] \succ 1/2[z_1] \oplus 1/2[z_2]$. Viewed as points in $\mathbb{R}_+^2$, we can rewrite this as $(1,0) \succ (1/2, 1/2)$. Any neighborhood of $(1,0)$ contains lotteries that are not strictly preferred to $(1/2, 1/2)$, and thus C is not satisfied. The preference relation also does not satisfy I ($[z_1] \succ [z_2]$ but $1/2[z_1] \oplus 1/2[z_2] \sim [z_2]$.)

Utility Representation

By Debreu's theorem we know that for any relation $\succsim$ defined on the space of lotteries that satisfies C, there is a utility representation U: $L(Z) \to \mathbb{R}$, continuous in the probabilities, such that $p \succsim q$ iff $U(p) \geq U(q)$. We will use the above axioms to isolate a family of preference relations that have a representation by a more structured utility function.

Theorem (vNM):

Let $\succsim$ be a preference relation over $L(Z)$ satisfying I and C. There are numbers $(v(z))_{z \in Z}$ such that

$$p \succsim q \text{ iff } U(p) = \Sigma_{z \in Z} p(z) v(z) \geq U(q) = \Sigma_{z \in Z} q(z) v(z).$$

Note the distinction between $U(p)$ (the utility number of the lottery p) and $v(z)$ (called the Bernoulli numbers or the vNM utilities). The function v is a utility function representing the preferences on Z and is the building block for the construction of $U(p)$, a utility function representing the preferences on $L(Z)$. We often refer to v as a vNM utility function representing the preferences $\succsim$ over $L(Z)$.

For the proof of the theorem, we need the following lemma:

Lemma:

Let $\succsim$ be a preference over $L(Z)$ satisfying Axiom I. Let $x, y \in Z$ such that $[x] \succ [y]$ and $1 \geq \alpha > \beta \geq 0$. Then

$$\alpha x \oplus (1 - \alpha) y \succ \beta x \oplus (1 - \beta) y.$$

Proof:

If either $\alpha = 1$ or $\beta = 0$, the claim is implied by I. Otherwise, by I, $\alpha x \oplus (1-\alpha) y \succ [y]$. Using I again we get: $\alpha x \oplus (1-\alpha) y \succ (\beta/\alpha)(\alpha x \oplus (1-\alpha) y) \oplus (1-\beta/\alpha)[y] = \beta x \oplus (1-\beta) y$.

Proof of the theorem:

Let M and m be a best and a worst certain lotteries in $L(Z)$.

Consider first the case that $M \sim m$. It follows from I^* that $p \sim m$ for any p and thus $p \sim q$ for all $p, q \in L(Z)$. Thus, any constant utility function represents $\succsim$. Choosing $v(z) = 0$ for all z, we have $\Sigma_{z \in Z} p(z) v(z) = 0$ for all $p \in L(Z)$.

Now consider the case that $M \succ m$. By C^* and the lemma, there is a single number $v(z) \in [0, 1]$ such that $v(z)M \oplus (1-v(z))m \sim [z]$. (In particular, $v(M) = 1$ and $v(m) = 0$). By I^* we obtain that

$$p \sim (\Sigma_{z \in Z} p(z)v(z))M \oplus (1 - \Sigma_{z \in Z} p(z)v(z))m.$$

And by the lemma $p \succsim q$ iff $\Sigma_{z \in Z} p(z)v(z) \geq \Sigma_{z \in Z} q(z)v(z)$.

The Uniqueness of vNM Utilities

The vNM utilities are unique up to positive affine transformation (namely, multiplication by a positive number and adding any scalar) and are not invariant to arbitrary monotonic transformation. Consider a preference relation $\succsim$ defined over $L(Z)$ and let $v(z)$ be the vNM utilities representing the preference relation. Of course, defining $w(z) = \alpha v(z) + \beta$ for all z (for some $\alpha > 0$ and some β), the utility function $W(p) = \Sigma_{z \in Z} p(z)w(z)$ also represents $\succsim$.

Furthermore, assume that $W(p) = \Sigma_z p(z)w(z)$ represents the preferences $\succsim$ as well. We will show that w must be a positive affine transformation of v. To see this, let $\alpha > 0$ and β satisfy

$$w(M) = \alpha v(M) + \beta \quad \text{and} \quad w(m) = \alpha v(m) + \beta$$

(the existence of $\alpha > 0$ and β is guaranteed by $v(M) > v(m)$ and $w(M) > w(m)$). For any $z \in Z$ there must be a number p such that $[z] \sim pM \oplus (1 - p)m$, so it must be that

$$\begin{aligned}
w(z) &= pw(M) + (1 - p)w(m) \\
&= p[\alpha v(M) + \beta] + (1 - p)[\alpha v(m) + \beta] \\
&= \alpha[pv(M) + (1 - p)v(m)] + \beta \\
&= \alpha v(z) + \beta.
\end{aligned}$$

The Dutch Book Argument

There are those who consider expected utility maximization to be a normative principle. One of the arguments made to support this view is the following Dutch book argument. Assume that $L_1 \succ L_2$ but that $\alpha L \oplus (1 - \alpha)L_2 \succ \alpha L \oplus (1 - \alpha)L_1$. We can perform the following trick on the decision maker:

1. Take $\alpha L \oplus (1 - \alpha)L_1$ (we can describe this as a contingency with random event E, which we both agree has probability $1 - \alpha$).

2. Take instead $\alpha L \oplus (1 - \alpha)L_2$, which you prefer (and you pay me something ...).
3. Let us agree to replace L_2 with L_1 in case E occurs (and you pay me something now).
4. Note that you hold $\alpha L \oplus (1 - \alpha)L_1$.
5. Let us start from the beginning ...

A Discussion of the Plausibility of the vNM Theory

Many experiments reveal systematic deviations from vNM assumptions. The most famous one is the *Allais paradox*. One version of it (see Kahneman and Tversky (1979)) is the following:

Choose first between

$$L_1 = 0.25[3,000] \oplus 0.75[0] \quad \text{and} \quad L_2 = 0.2[4,000] \oplus 0.8[0]$$

and then choose between

$$L_3 = 1[3,000] \quad \text{and} \quad L_4 = 0.8[4,000] \oplus 0.2[0].$$

Note that $L_1 = 0.25L_3 \oplus 0.75[0]$ and $L_2 = 0.25L_4 \oplus 0.75[0]$. Axiom I requires that the preference between L_1 and L_2 be respectively the same as that between L_3 and L_4. However, in experiments a majority of people express the preferences $L_1 \prec L_2$ and an even larger majority express the preferences $L_3 \succ L_4$. This phenomenon persists even among graduate students in economics. Among about 228 graduate students at Princeton, Tel Aviv, and NYU, although they were asked to respond to the above two choice problems on line one after the other, 68% chose L_2 while 78% chose L_3. This means that at least 46% of the students violated property I.

The Allais example demonstrates (again) the sensitivity of preference to the framing of the alternatives. When the lotteries L_1 and L_2 are presented as they are above, most prefer L_2. But, if we present L_1 and L_2 as the compound lotteries $L_1 = 0.25L_3 \oplus 0.75[0]$ and $L_2 = 0.25L_4 \oplus 0.75[0]$, most subjects prefer L_1 to L_2.

Comment:

In the proof of the vNM theorem we have seen that the independence axiom implies that if one is indifferent between z and z', one is also indifferent between z and any lottery with z and z' as its prizes. This is not plausible in cases in which one takes into account the fairness of the random process that selects the prizes. For example, consider a parent in a situation where he has one gift and two children, M and Y (guess why I chose these letters). His options are to choose a lottery $L(p)$ that will award M the gift with probability p and Y with probability $1 - p$. The parent does not favor one child over the other. The vNM approach "predicts" that he will be indifferent among all lotteries that determine who receives the gift, while common sense tells us usually he will strictly prefer $L(1/2)$.

Subjective Expected Utility (de Finetti's)

In the above discussion, a lottery was a description of the probabilities with which each of the prizes is obtained. In many contexts, an alternative induces an uncertain consequence that depends on certain events though the probabilities of those events are not given. The attitude of the decision maker to an alternative will depend on his assessment of the likelihoods of those events. In this section, we will demonstrate the basic idea of eliciting liabilities from preferences.

The major work in this area is Savage's model. However, Savage's axiomatization is quite complicated, and we will make do here with a very simple model (due de Finetti) that demonstrates an important component of the approach.

In this model, the notion of a lottery is replaced by a notion of a bet. Think about someone betting on a race with K horses (and, needless to say, the set of horses represents an exhaustive list of exclusive events). A bet is a vector $(x_1, \ldots, x_K)$ with the interpretation that if horse k wins the decision maker receives $\$x_k$ (x_k can be any real number). Let B be the set of all bets. Assume that the better has a preference relation on B.

We will consider three properties of the preference relation:

- Continuity: The standard continuity property we use on the Euclidean space.
- Weak Monotonicity: If $x_k > y_k$, then $x \succ y$.
- Additivity: If $x \succsim y$, then $x + z \succsim y + z$ for all z. (Note that this implies that if $x \succ y$, then $x + z \succ y + z$ for all z.)

A possible interpretation of the additivity property is as follows: Assume that the wealth of the decision maker has two components: One of them, z, is independent of the choice between the different bets. The other depends on the bet he chooses: x or y. Additivity states that the attitude of the decision maker to the bets x and y is independent of z.

Claim:

A preference relation $\succsim$ satisfies Continuity, Weak Monotonicity, and Additivity if and only if there is a probability vector $(\pi_1, \ldots, \pi_K)$ such that $x \succsim y$ if and only if $\sum \pi_k x_k \geq \sum \pi_k y_k$.

Proof:

Actually, we have already proved this claim for $K = 2$ (see Problem Set 2 Question 5). We will prove it now for an arbitrary K, using another technique:

A preference relation represented by $\sum \pi_k x_k$ obviously satisfies all the three properties.

In the other direction, assume that $\succsim$ satisfies the three properties. First, consider the two sets $U = \{x \mid x \succsim 0\}$ and $D = \{x \mid 0 \succ x\}$. Both are nonempty. By continuity U is closed and D is open. Furthermore, both are convex. To see that U is convex, note that if $x \succsim 0$ and $y \succsim 0$, then by Additivity $x + y \succsim y \succsim 0$. Furthermore, by Additivity if $x \succsim 0$, then for all $\lambda = m/2^n$ we have $\lambda x \succsim 0$ and by Continuity $\lambda x \succsim 0$ for all λ. By the definition of a preference relation, the sets U and D provide a partition of $\mathbb{R}^K$, that is, $U \cup D = \mathbb{R}^K$ and $U \cap D = \emptyset$.

Now use a separation theorem to conclude that there exists a non-zero vector $\pi = (\pi_1, \ldots, \pi_K)$ and a number c such that $U = \{x \mid \pi x \geq c\}$ and $D = \{x \mid \pi x < c\}$. By Weak Monotonicity, it is easy to see that $c = 0$, $\pi \neq 0$, and $\pi_k \geq 0$ for all k. Thus, without loss of generality we can assume $\sum \pi_k = 1$.

Now, $x \succsim y$ if and only if $x - y \succsim 0$ if and only if $\pi(x - y) \geq 0$ if and only if $\pi x \geq \pi y$.

Bibliographic Notes

Recommended readings. Kreps 1990, 72–81 and 115–122; Mas-Colell et al. 1995, chapter 6, A–B.

Expected utility theory is based on von Neumann and Morgenstern (1944). Kreps (1988) has an excellent presentation of the material. For a recent survey of theories of decision under uncertainty, see Gilboa (2009). Machina (1987) remains a recommended survey of alternative theories. Kahneman and Tversky (1979) is a must read for psychological criticism of expected utility theory. More recent material is covered in Kahneman and Tversky (2000).

Problem Set 8

Problem 1. (*Standard*)
Consider the following preference relations that were described in the text: "the size of the support" and "comparing the most likely prize".

a. Check carefully whether they satisfy axioms I and C.
b. These preference relations are not immune to a certain "framing problem". Explain.

Problem 2. (*Standard. Based on Markowitz (1959).*)
One way to construct preferences over lotteries with monetary prizes is by evaluating each lottery L on the basis of two numbers: $Ex(L)$, the expectation of L, and $var(L)$, L's variance. Such a construction may or may not be consistent with vNM assumptions.

a. Show that the function $u(L) = Ex(L) - (1/4)var(L)$ induces a preference relation that is not consistent with the vNM assumptions. (For example, consider the mixtures of each of the lotteries $[1]$ and $0.5[0] \oplus 0.5[4]$ with the lottery $0.5[0] \oplus 0.5[2]$.)
b. Show that the utility function $u(L) = Ex(L) - (Ex(L))^2 - var(L)$ is consistent with vNM assumptions.

Problem 3. (*Standard*)
A decision maker has a preference relation $\succsim$ over the space of lotteries $L(Z)$ having a set of prizes Z. On Sunday he learns that on Monday he will be told whether he has to choose between L_1 and L_2 (probability $1 > \alpha > 0$) or between L_3 and L_4 (probability $1 - \alpha$). He will make his choice at that time.

Let us compare between two possible approaches the decision maker can take.

Approach 1: He delays his decision to Monday ("why bother with the decision now when I can make up my mind tomorrow ...").

Approach 2: He makes a contingent decision on Sunday regarding what he will do on Monday, that is, he decides what to do if he faces the choice between L_1 and L_2 and what to do if he faces the choice between L_3 and L_4 ("On Monday morning I will be so busy ...").

a. Formulate Approach 2 as a choice between lotteries.
b. Show that if the preferences of the decision maker satisfy the independence axiom, then his choice under Approach 2 will always be the same as under Approach 1.

Problem 4. (*Difficult*)

A decision maker is to choose an action from a set A. The set of consequences is Z. For every action $a \in A$ the consequence z^* is realized with probability α, and any $z \in Z - \{z^*\}$ is realized with probability $r(a, z) = (1 - \alpha)q(a, z)$.

   a. Assume that after making his choice he is told that z^* will not occur and is given a chance to change his decision. Show that if the decision maker obeys the Bayesian updating rule and follows vNM axioms, he will not change his decision.
   b. Give an example where a decision maker who follows a nonexpected utility preference relation or obeys a non-Bayesian updating rule is not time consistent.

Problem 5. (*Standard*)

Assume there is a finite number of income levels. An income distribution specifies the proportion of individuals at each level. Thus, an income distribution has the same mathematical structure as a lottery. Consider the binary relation "one distribution is more egalitarian than another".

   a. Why is the von Neumann–Morgenstern independence axiom inappropriate for characterizing this type of relation?
   b. Suggest and formulate a property that is appropriate, in your opinion, as an axiom for this relation. Give two examples of preference relations that satisfy this property.

Problem 6. (*Difficult. Based on Miyamoto, Wakker, Bleichrodt, and Peters (1998).*)

A decision maker faces a trade-off between longevity and quality of life. His preference relation ranks lotteries on the set of all certain outcomes of the form (q, t) defined as "a life of quality q and length t" (where q and t are nonnegative numbers). Assume that the preference relation satisfies von Neumann–Morgenstern assumptions and that it also satisfies the following:

   1. There is indifference between any two certain lotteries $[(q, 0)]$ and $[(q', 0)]$.
   2. Risk neutrality with respect to life duration: An uncertain lifetime of expected duration T is equally preferred to a certain lifetime duration T when q is held fixed.
   3. Whatever quality of life, the longer the life the better.

   a. Show that the preference relation derived from maximizing the expectation of the function $v(q)t$, where $v(q) > 0$ for all q satisfies the assumptions.

b. Show that all preference relations satisfying the above assumptions can
be represented by an expected utility function of the form $v(q)t$, where
v is a positive function.

Problem 7. (*Food for thought*)

Consider a decision maker who systematically calculates that $2 + 3 = 6$. Construct a "money pump" argument against him. Discuss the argument.

Risk Aversion

Lotteries with Monetary Prizes

We proceed to a discussion of a decision maker satisfying vNM assumptions where the space of prizes Z is a set of real numbers and $a \in Z$ is interpreted as "receiving $\$a$". Note that in Lecture 8 we assumed the set Z is finite; here, in contrast, we apply the expected utility approach to a set that is infinite. For simplicity we will still consider only lotteries with finite support. In other words, in this lecture, a lottery p is a real function on Z such that $p(z) \geq 0$ for all $z \in Z$, and there is a finite set Y such that $\sum_{z \in Y} p(z) = 1$. It is easy to extend the axiomatization presented in Lecture 8 for this case.

We will make special assumptions that fit the interpretation of the members of Z as sums of money. Recall $[x]$ denotes the lottery that yields the prize x with certainty. We will say that $\succsim$ satisfies *monotonicity* if $a > b$ implies $[a] \succ [b]$.

From here on we focus the discussion on preference relations over the space of lotteries for which there is a continuous function u, such that the preference relation over lotteries is represented by the function $Eu(p) = \sum_{z \in Z} p(z)u(z)$. The function Eu assigns to the lottery p the expectation of the random variable that receives the value $u(x)$ with a probability $p(x)$.

The following argument, called the *St. Petersburg Paradox*, is sometimes presented as a justification for assuming that vNM utility functions are bounded. Assume that a decision maker has an unbounded vNM utility function u. Consider playing the following "trick" on him:

1. Assume he possesses wealth x_0.
2. Offer him a lottery that will reduce his wealth to 0 with probability $1/2$ and will increase his wealth to x_1 with probability $1/2$ so that $u(x_0) < [u(0) + u(x_1)]/2$. By the unboundedness of u, there exists such an x_1.

3. If he loses, you are happy. If he is lucky, a moment before you give
   him x_1, offer him a lottery that will give him x_2 with probability $1/2$
   and 0 otherwise, where x_2 is such that $u(x_1) < [u(0) + u(x_2)]/2$.
4. And so on ...

Our (poor) decision maker will find himself with wealth 0 with
probability 1!

First-Order Stochastic Domination

We say that p *first-order stochastically dominates* q (written as pD_1q)
if $p \succsim q$ for any $\succsim$ on $L(Z)$ satisfying vNM assumptions as well as
monotonicity in money. That is, pD_1q if $Eu(p) \geq Eu(q)$ for all increasing u. This is the simplest example of questions of the type: "Given a set
of preference relations on $L(Z)$, for what pairs $p, q \in L(Z)$ is $p \succsim q$ for
all $\succsim$ in the set?" In the problem set you will discuss another example
of this kind of question.

Obviously, pD_1q if the entire support of p is to the right of the entire
support of q. But we are concerned with a more interesting condition
on a pair of lotteries p and q, one that will be not only sufficient but
also necessary for p to first-order stochastically dominate q.

For any lottery p and a number x, define $G(p, x) = \sum_{z \geq x} p(z)$ (the
probability that the lottery p yields a prize at least as high as x). Denote
by $F(p, x)$ the cumulative distribution function of p, that is, $F(p, x) = \sum_{z \leq x} p(z)$.

Claim:

pD_1q iff for all x, $G(p, x) \geq G(q, x)$ (alternatively, pD_1q iff for all x,
$F(p, x) \leq F(q, x)$). (See fig. 9.1.)

Proof:

Let $x_0 < x_1 < x_2 < \ldots < x_K$ be the prizes in the union of the supports
of p and q. First, note the following alternative expression for $Eu(p)$:

$$Eu(p) = \sum_{k \geq 0} p(x_k)u(x_k) = u(x_0) + \sum_{k \geq 1} G(p, x_k)(u(x_k) - u(x_{k-1})).$$

Now, if $G(p, x_k) \geq G(q, x_k)$ for all k, then for all increasing u,

$$Eu(p) = u(x_0) + \sum_{k \geq 1} G(p, x_k)(u(x_k) - u(x_{k-1})) \geq$$

$$u(x_0) + \sum_{k \geq 1} G(q, x_k)(u(x_k) - u(x_{k-1})) = Eu(q).$$

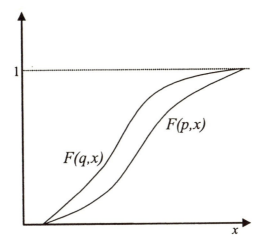

Figure 9.1
p first-order stochastically dominates q.

Conversely, if there exists k^* for which $G(p, x_{k^*}) < G(q, x_{k^*})$, then we can find an increasing function u so that $Eu(p) < Eu(q)$, by setting $u(x_{k^*}) - u(x_{k^*-1})$ to be very large and the other increments to be very small.

Risk Aversion

We say that $\succsim$ is *risk averse* if for any lottery p, $[Ep] \succsim p$.

We will see now that for a decision maker with preferences $\succsim$ obeying the vNM axioms, risk aversion is closely related to the concavity of the vNM utility function representing $\succsim$.

First recall some basic properties of concave functions (if you are not familiar with those properties, this will be an excellent opportunity for you to prove them yourself):

1. An increasing and concave function must be continuous (but not necessarily differentiable).
2. The *Jensen Inequality*: If u is concave, then for any finite sequence $(\alpha_k)_{k=1,\dots,K}$ of positive numbers that sum up to 1, $u(\sum_{k=1}^{K} \alpha_k x_k) \geq \sum_{k=1}^{K} \alpha_k u(x_k)$.
3. The *Three Strings Lemma*: For any $a < b < c$ we have

$$[u(c) - u(b)]/(c - b) \leq [u(c) - u(a)]/(c - a) \leq [u(b) - u(a)]/(b - a).$$

4. If u is twice differentiable, then for any $a < c$, $u'(a) \geq u'(c)$, and thus $u''(x) \leq 0$ for all x.

Claim:

Let $\succsim$ be a preference on $L(Z)$ represented by the vNM utility function u. The preference relation $\succsim$ is risk averse iff u is concave.

Proof:

Assume that u is concave. By the Jensen Inequality, for any lottery p, $u(E(p)) \geq Eu(p)$ and thus $[E(p)] \succsim p$.

Assume that $\succsim$ is risk averse and that u represents $\succsim$. For all $\alpha \in (0,1)$ and for all $x, y \in Z$, we have by risk aversion $[\alpha x + (1-\alpha)y] \succsim \alpha x \oplus (1-\alpha)y$ and thus $u(\alpha x + (1-\alpha)y) \geq \alpha u(x) + (1-\alpha)u(y)$, that is, u is concave.

Certainty Equivalence and the Risk Premium

Let $E(p)$ be the expectation of the lottery p, that is, $E(p) = \sum_{z \in Z} p(z)z$. Given a preference relation $\succsim$ over the space $L(Z)$, the *certainty equivalence* of a lottery p, $CE(p)$, is a prize satisfying $[CE(p)] \sim p$. (Verify the existence of $CE(p)$ is guaranteed by assuming that $\succsim$ is monotonic in the sense that if $pD_1 q$, then $p \succ q$ and continuous in the sense that the sets $\{c \in \mathbb{R} \mid [c] \succ p\}$ and $\{c \in \mathbb{R} \mid p \succ [c]\}$ are open). The *risk premium* of p is the difference $R(P) = E(p) - CE(p)$. By definition, the preferences are risk averse if and only if $R(p) \geq 0$ for all p. (See fig. 9.2.)

The "More Risk Averse" Relation

We wish to formalize the statement "one decision maker *is more risk averse* than another". To understand the logic of the following definitions let us start with an analogous phrase: "A is more war averse than B". One possible meaning of this phrase is that whenever A is ready to go to war, B is as well. Another possible meaning is that when facing the threat of war, A is ready to agree to a less attractive compromise than B is. (Note that the assumption that A and B share the same concepts of "war" and "peace" is implicit in these interpretations.) The following two definitions are analogous to these two interpretations. (See fig. 9.3.)

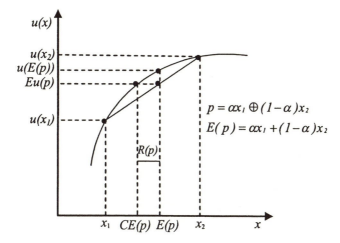

Figure 9.2
CE and risk premium.

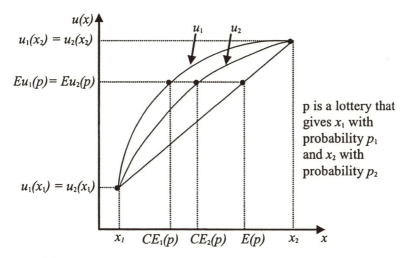

Figure 9.3
1 is more risk averse than 2.

1. The preference relation $\succsim_1$ *is more risk averse than* $\succsim_2$ if, for any lottery p and degenerate lottery c, $p \succsim_1 c$ implies that $p \succsim_2 c$.

In case the preferences are monotonic, we have a second definition:

2. The preference relation $\succsim_1$ *is more risk averse than* $\succsim_2$ if $CE_1(p) \leq CE_2(p)$ for all p.

In case the preferences satisfy vNM assumptions, we have a third definition:

3. Let u_1 and u_2 be vNM utility functions representing $\succsim_1$ and $\succsim_2$, respectively. The preference relation $\succsim_1$ is more risk averse than $\succsim_2$ if the function φ, defined by $u_1(t) = \varphi(u_2(t))$, is concave.

Note that definition (1) is meaningful in any space of prizes (not only those in which consequences are numerical) and for a general set of preferences (and not only those satisfying vNM assumptions).

Claim:

If both $\succsim_1$ and $\succsim_2$ are preference relations on $L(Z)$ represented by increasing and continuous vNM utility functions, then the three definitions are equivalent.

Proof:

- If (2), then (1).
  Assume (2). If $p \succsim_1 [c]$, then by transitivity $[CE_1(p)] \succsim_1 [c]$ and by the monotonicity of $\succsim_1$ we have $CE_1(p) \geq c$, which implies also that $CE_2(p) \geq c$, and by transitivity of $\succsim_2$, $p \succsim_2 [c]$.
- If (3) then (2).
  By definition, $Eu_i(p) = u_i(CE_i(p))$. Thus, $CE_i(p) = u_i^{-1}(Eu_i(p))$. If $\varphi = u_1 u_2^{-1}$ is concave, then by the Jensen Inequality:

$$u_1(CE_2(p)) = u_1(u_2^{-1}(Eu_2(p))) = \varphi\left(\sum_x p(x)u_2(x)\right) \geq$$

$$\left(\sum_x p(x)\varphi u_2(x)\right) = \sum_x p(x)u_1(x) = E(u_1(p)) = u_1(CE_1(p)).$$

  Since u_1 is increasing, $CE_2(p) \geq CE_1(p)$.
- If (1), then (3).
  Consider three numbers $u_2(x) < u_2(y) < u_2(z)$ in the range of u_2 and let $\lambda \in (0,1)$ satisfy $u_2(y) = \lambda u_2(x) + (1-\lambda)u_2(z)$. Let us prove that $u_1(y) \geq \lambda u_1(x) + (1-\lambda)u_1(z)$.
  If $u_1(y) < \lambda u_1(x) + (1-\lambda)u_1(z)$, then for some $\mu > \lambda$ we have both $u_1(y) < \mu u_1(x) + (1-\mu)u_1(z)$ and $u_2(y) > \mu u_2(x) + (1-\mu)u_2(z)$, that is, $y \prec_1 \mu x \oplus (1-\mu)z$ and $y \succ_2 \mu x \oplus (1-\mu)z$, which contradicts (1). Thus, $y \succsim_1 \lambda x \oplus (1-\lambda)z$ and $u_1(y) \geq \lambda u_1(x) + (1-\lambda)u_1(z)$, that is, $\varphi(u_2(y)) \geq \lambda\varphi(u_2(x)) + (1-\lambda) \times \varphi(u_2(z))$. Thus, φ is concave.

The Coefficient of Absolute Risk Aversion

The following is another definition of the relation "more risk averse" applied to the case in which vNM utility functions are twice differentiable:

4. Let u_1 and u_2 be twice differentiable vNM utility functions representing $\succsim_1$ and $\succsim_2$, respectively. The preference relation $\succsim_1$ *is more risk averse than* $\succsim_2$ if $r_1(x) \geq r_2(x)$ for all x, where $r_i(x) = -u_i''(x)/u_i'(x)$.

The number $r(x) = -u''(x)/u'(x)$ is called the *coefficient of absolute risk aversion* of u at x. We will see that a higher coefficient of absolute risk aversion means a more risk-averse decision maker.

To see that (3) and (4) are equivalent, note the following chain of equivalences:

- Definition (3) (i.e., $u_1 u_2^{-1}$ is concave) is satisfied iff
- the function $d/dt[u_1(u_2^{-1}(t))]$ is nonincreasing in t iff
- $u_1'(u_2^{-1}(t))/u_2'(u_2^{-1}(t))$ is nonincreasing in t (since $(\varphi^{-1})'(t) = 1/\varphi'(\varphi^{-1}(t))$) iff
- $u_1'(x)/u_2'(x)$ is nonincreasing in x (since $u_2^{-1}(t)$ is increasing in t) iff
- $log\,[(u_1'/u_2')(x)] = log\,u_1'(x) - log\,u_2'(x)$ is nonincreasing in x iff
- the derivative of $log\,u_1'(x) - log\,u_2'(x)$ is nonpositive iff
- $r_2(x) - r_1(x) \leq 0$ for all x where $r_i(x) = -u_i''(x)/u_i'(x)$ iff
- definition (4) is satisfied.

For a better understanding of the coefficient of absolute risk aversion, it is useful to look at the preferences on the restricted domain of lotteries of the type $(x_1, x_2) = px_1 \oplus (1-p)x_2$, where the probability p is fixed. Denote by u a continuously differentiable vNM utility function that represents a risk-averse preference.

Let $x_2 = \psi(x_1)$ be the function describing the indifference curve through (t, t), the point representing $[t]$. Thus, $\psi(t) = t$.

It follows from risk aversion that all lotteries with expectation t, that is, all lotteries on the line $\{(x_1, x_2)|\ px_1 + (1-p)x_2 = t\}$, are not above the indifference curve through (t, t). Thus, $\psi'(t) = -p/(1-p)$.

By definition of u as a vNM utility function representing the preferences over the space of lotteries, we have $pu(x_1) + (1-p)u(\psi(x_1)) = u(t)$. Taking the derivative with respect to x_1, we obtain $pu'(x_1) + (1-p)u'(\psi(x_1))\psi'(x_1) = 0$. Taking the derivative with respect to x_1 once again, we obtain

$$pu''(x_1) + (1-p)u''(\psi(x_1))[\psi'(x_1)]^2 + (1-p)u'(\psi(x_1))\psi''(x_1) = 0.$$

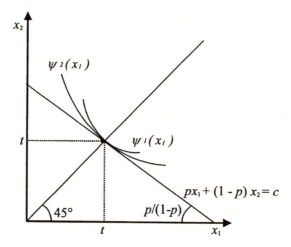

Figure 9.4
1 is more risk averse than 2.

At $x_1 = t$ we have

$$pu''(t) + u''(t)p^2/(1-p) + (1-p)u'(t)\psi''(t) = 0.$$

Therefore,

$$\psi''(t) = -u''(t)/u'(t)[p/(1-p)^2] = r(t)[p/(1-p)^2].$$

Note that on this restricted space of lotteries, $\succsim_1$ is more risk averse than $\succsim_2$ in the sense of definition (1) iff the indifference curve of $\succsim_1$ through (t, t), denoted by ψ_1, is never below the indifference curve of $\succsim_2$ through (t, t), denoted by ψ_2. Combined with $\psi_1'(t) = \psi_2'(t)$, we obtain that $\psi_1''(t) \geq \psi_2''(t)$ and thus $r_2(t) \leq r_1(t)$. (See fig. 9.4.)

The Doctrine of Consequentialism

Conduct the following "thought experiment":
You have $2,000 in your bank account. You have to choose between

1. a sure loss of $500
   and
2. a lottery in which you lose $1,000 with probability $1/2$ and lose 0 with probability $1/2$.

What is your choice?

Now assume that you have $1,000 in your account and that you have to choose between

3. a certain gain of $500
   and
4. a lottery in which you win $1,000 with probability 1/2 and win 0 with probability 1/2.

What is your choice?

Of Kahneman and Tversky (1979)'s subjects, in the first case 69% preferred the lottery to the certain loss (i.e., they chose (2)), while in the second case 84% preferred the certain gain of $500 (i.e., they chose (3)). These results indicate that about half of the population exhibit a preference for (2) over (1) and (3) over (4). Such a preference does not conflict with expected utility theory if we interpret a prize to reflect a "monetary change". However, if we assume that the decision maker takes the final wealth levels to be his prizes, we have a problem: in terms of final wealth levels, both choice problems are between a certain $1,500 and a lottery that yields $2,000 or $1,000 with probability 1/2 each.

Incidentally, in the results from my site (using a somewhat different framing of the question) only 34% of the subjects chose (2) over (1). When the dollars were replaced with lives, the proportion of subjects who chose the lottery increased to 54%.

Nevertheless, in the economic literature it is usually assumed that a decision maker's preferences over wealth changes are induced from his preferences with regard to "final wealth levels". Formally, when starting with wealth w, denote by $\succsim_w$ the decision maker's preferences over lotteries in which the prizes are interpreted as "changes" in wealth. By the *doctrine of consequentialism* all relations $\succsim_w$ are derived from the same preference relation, $\succsim$, defined over the "final wealth levels" by $p \succsim_w q$ iff $w + p \succsim w + q$ (where $w + p$ is the lottery that awards a prize $w + x$ with probability $p(x)$). If $\succsim$ is represented by a vNM utility function u, this doctrine implies that for all w, the function $v_w(x) = u(w + x)$ is a vNM utility function representing the preferences $\succsim_w$.

Invariance to Wealth

We say that the preference relation $\succsim$ exhibits *invariance to wealth* (in the literature it is often called *constant absolute risk aversion*) if the induced preference relation $\succsim_w$ is independent of w, that is, $(w + L_1) \succsim (w + L_2)$ is true or false independent of w.

We will see that if u is a continuous vNM utility function representing preferences $\succsim$, which exhibit risk aversion and invariance to wealth, then u must be exponential or linear.

Let us first confine ourselves to the $\Delta - grid$ prize space, $Z = \{x \mid x = n\Delta$ for some integer $n\}$. This domain has a special meaning when we take Δ to be the smallest (indivisible) unit of money.

By continuity of u, for any wealth level x there is a number q such that $(1 - q)(x - \Delta) \oplus q(x + \Delta) \sim x$. By the invariance to wealth, q is independent of x. Thus, we have $u(x + \Delta) - u(x) = ((1 - q)/q)[u(x) - u(x - \Delta)]$ for all x. This means that the increments in the function u, when x is increased by Δ, constitute a geometric sequence with a factor of $(1 - q)/q$ (where q might depend on Δ). Using the formula for the sum of a geometric sequence, we conclude that the function u, defined on the $\Delta - grid$, must equal $a - b(\frac{1-q}{q})^{\frac{x}{\Delta}}$ or $a + b\frac{x}{\Delta}$ for some a and b.

Note, that the comparisons of the lottery $[0]$ with the simple lotteries involving a gain and loss of Δ are sufficient to characterize a unique preference relation that is consistent with: (i) the doctrine of consequentialism, (ii) the assumption that the preferences regarding lotteries over changes in wealth are independent of the initial wealth, and (iii) the expected utility assumptions regarding the space of lotteries in which the prizes are the final wealth levels. Many researchers have tried to reveal the decision maker's preferences experimentally under these assumptions using the question: "What is the probability q that will make you indifferent between a gain of $\$\Delta$ with probability q and a loss of $\$\Delta$ with probability $1 - q$?" The results vary. Moreover, asking individuals different questions of this type is likely to lead to inconsistent answers.

Let us now return to the case of $Z = \mathbb{R}$ and look at the preferences over the restricted space of all lotteries of the type $(x_1, x_2) = px_1 \oplus (1 - p)x_2$ for some arbitrary fixed probability $p \in (0, 1)$. Denote the indifference curve through (t, t) by $x_2 = \psi_t(x_1)$. Thus, $[t] \sim px_1 \oplus (1 - p)\psi_t(x_1)$. Since $\succsim$ exhibits constant absolute risk aversion, it must be that $[0] \sim p(x_1 - t) \oplus (1 - p)(\psi_t(x_1) - t)$ and thus $\psi_0(x_1 - t) = \psi_t(x_1) - t$, or $\psi_t(x_1) = \psi_0(x_1 - t) + t$. In other words, the indifference curve through (t, t) is the indifference curve through $(0, 0)$ shifted in the direction of (t, t).

Assuming that the function u is differentiable, we derive that $\psi_t''(t) = \psi_0''(0)$. We have already seen that $\psi_t''(t) = -[p/(1-p)^2][u_i''(t)/u_i'(t)]$, and thus there exists a constant α such that $-u''(t)/u'(t) = \alpha$ for all t. This implies that $[log\, u'(t)]' = -\alpha$ for all t and $log\, u'(t) = -\alpha t + \beta$ for some β. It follows that $u'(t) = e^{-\alpha t + \beta}$. If $\alpha = 0$, the function $u(t)$ must be linear (implying risk neutrality). If $\alpha \neq 0$, it must be that $u(t) = ce^{-\alpha t} + d$ for some c and d.

To conclude, if u is a vNM continuous utility function representing preferences that are monotonic and exhibit both risk aversion and invariance to wealth, then u is an affine transformation of either the function t or a function $-e^{-\alpha t}$ (with $\alpha > 0$).

Critique of the Doctrine of Consequentialism

Denote by $1/2(-D) \oplus 1/2(+G)$ the lottery in which there is an equal probability of gaining \$$G$ and losing \$$D$. Consider a risk-averse decision maker who likes money, obeys expected utility theory, and adheres to the doctrine of consequentialism. Rabin (2000) noted that if such a decision maker turns down the lottery $L = 1/2(-10) \oplus 1/2(+11)$, at any wealth level between \$0 and \$5,000 (a quite plausible assumption), then at the wealth level \$4,000 he must reject the lottery $1/2(-100) \oplus 1/2(+71,000)$ (a quite ridiculous conclusion).

The intuition for this observation is quite simple. Since L is rejected at $w + 10$, we have that $u(w + 10) \geq [u(w + 21) + u(w)]/2$. Therefore, $u(w + 10) - u(w) \geq u(w + 21) - u(w + 10)$ or

$$\frac{10}{11} \left(\frac{u(w + 10) - u(w)}{10} \right) \geq \frac{u(w + 21) - u(w + 10)}{11}.$$

By the concavity of u the right-hand side of this equation is at least as high as the marginal utility at $w + 21$, whereas the left-hand side is at most $10/11$ times the marginal utility at w. Thus the marginal utility at $w + 21$ is at most $10/11$ the marginal utility at w.

Thus, the sequence of marginal utilities within the domain of wealth levels in which L is rejected falls at least in a geometric rate. This implies that for the lottery $1/2(-D) \oplus 1/2(+G)$ to be accepted even for a relatively low D, one would need a huge G.

What conclusions should we draw from this observation? In my opinion, in contrast to what some scholars claim, this is not a refutation of expected utility theory. Rabin's argument relies on the doctrine of consequentialism, which is not a part of expected utility theory. Expected utility theory is invariant to the interpretation of the prizes. Independently of the theory of decision making under uncertainty that we use, the set of prizes should be the set of consequences in the mind of the decision maker. Thus, it is equally reasonable to assume the consequences are "wealth changes" or "final wealth levels".

I treat Rabin's argument as further evidence of the empirically problematic nature of the doctrine of consequentialism according to which the decision maker makes *all* decisions having in mind a preference relation over *the same* set of final consequences. It also demonstrates how carefully we should tread when trying to estimate real-life agents' utility functions. The practice of estimating an economic agent's risk aversion parameters for small lotteries might lead to misleading conclusions if such estimates are used to characterize the decision maker's preferences regarding lotteries over large sums.

Bibliographic Notes

Recommended readings. Kreps 1990, 81–98; Mas-Colell et al. 1995, chapter 6, C–D.

The measures of risk aversion are taken from Arrow (1970) and Pratt (1964). For the psychological literature discussed here, see Kahneman and Tversky (1979) and Kahneman and Tversky (2000).

The St. Petersburg Paradox was suggested by Daniel Bernoulli in 1738 (see Bernoulli (1954)). The notion of stochastic domination was introduced into the economic literature by Rothschild and Stiglitz (1970). Rabin's argument is based on Rabin (2000).

Problem Set 9

Problem 1. (*Standard*)

    a. Show that a sequence of numbers $(a_1, \ldots, a_k)$ satisfies that $\sum a_k x_k \geq 0$ for all vectors $(x_1, \ldots, x_k)$ such that $x_k > 0$ for all k iff $a_k \geq 0$ for all k.

    b. Show that a sequence of numbers $(a_1, \ldots, a_k)$ satisfies that $\sum a_k x_k \geq 0$ for all vectors $(x_1, \ldots, x_k)$ such that $x_1 > x_2 > \ldots > x_K > x_{K+1} = 0$ iff $\sum_{k=1}^{l} a_k \geq 0$ for all l.

Problem 2. (*Standard. Based on Rothschild and Stiglitz (1970).*)

We say that p *second-order stochastically dominates* q and denote this by pD_2q if $p \succsim q$ for all preferences $\succsim$ satisfying the vNM assumptions, monotonicity, *and* risk aversion.

    a. Explain why pD_1q implies pD_2q.

    b. Let p and ε be lotteries. Define $p + \varepsilon$ to be the lottery that yields the prize t with the probability $\Sigma_{\alpha+\beta=t}p(\alpha)\varepsilon(\beta)$. Interpret $p + \varepsilon$. Show that if ε is a lottery with expectation 0, then for all p, $pD_2(p+\varepsilon)$.

    c. (More difficult) Show that pD_2q if and only if for all $t < K$, $\Sigma_{k=0}^{t}$ $[G(p, x_{k+1}) - G(q, x_{k+1})][x_{k+1} - x_k] \geq 0$ where $x_0 < \ldots < x_K$ are all the prizes in the support of either p or q and $G(p, x) = \Sigma_{z \geq x}p(z)$.

Problem 3. (*Standard. Based on Slovic and Lichtenstein (1968).*)

Consider a phenomenon called *preference reversal*. Let $L_1 = 8/9[\$4] \oplus 1/9[\$0]$ and $L_2 = 1/9[\$40] \oplus 8/9[\$0]$.

    Discuss the phenomenon that many people prefer L_1 to L_2, but when asked to evaluate the certainty equivalence of these lotteries, they attach a lower value to L_1 than to L_2.

Problem 4. (*Standard*)

Consider a consumer's preference relation over K-tuples describing quantities of K uncertain assets. Denote the random return on the k'th asset by Z_k. Assume that the random variables $(Z_1, \ldots, Z_K)$ are independent and take positive values with probability 1. If the consumer buys the combination of assets $(x_1, \ldots, x_K)$ and if the vector of realized returns is $(z_1, \ldots, z_K)$, then the consumer's total wealth is $\sum_{k=1}^{K} x_k z_k$. Assume that the consumer satisfies vNM assumptions, that is, there is a function v (over the sum of his returns) so that he maximizes the expected value of v. Assume that v is increasing and concave. The consumer preferences over the space of the lotteries induce preferences on the space of investments. Show that the induced preferences are monotonic and convex.

Problem 5. (*Standard. Based on Rubinstein (2002).*)
Adam lives in the Garden of Eden and eats only apples. Time in the garden is discrete ($t = 1, 2, \ldots$) and apples are eaten only in discrete units. Adam possesses preferences over the set of streams of apple consumption. Assume that:

a. Adam likes to eat up to 2 apples a day and cannot bear to eat 3 apples a day.
b. Adam is impatient. He would be delighted to increase his consumption on day t from 0 to 1 or from 1 to 2 apples at the expense of an apple he is promised a day later.
c. In any day in which he does not have an apple, he prefers to get 1 apple immediately in exchange for 2 apples tomorrow.
d. Adam expects to live for 120 years.

Show that if (poor) Adam is offered a stream of 2 apples starting in day 4 for the rest of his expected life, he would be willing to exchange that offer for 1 apple right away.

Problem 6. (*Moderately difficult. Based on Yaari (1987).*)
In this problem you will encounter Quiggin and Yaari's functional, one of the main alternatives to expected utility theory.

Recall that expected utility can be written as $U(p) = \sum_{k=1}^{K} p(z_k) u(z_k)$ where $z_0 < z_1 < \ldots < z_K$ are the prizes in the support of p. Let $W(p) = \sum_{k=1}^{K} f(G_p(z_k))[z_k - z_{k-1}]$, where $f : [0, 1] \to [0, 1]$ is a continuous increasing function and $G_p(z_k) = \sum_{j \geq k} p(z_j)$. ($p(z)$ is the probability that the lottery p yields z and G_p is the "anti-distribution" of p.)

a. The literature often refers to W as the dual expected utility operator. In what sense is W dual to U?
b. Show that W induces a preference relation on $L(z)$ that satisfies the continuity axiom but may not satisfy the independence axiom.
c. What are the difficulties with a functional form of the type $\sum_z f(p(z)) u(z)$? (See Handa (1977).)

Problem 7. (*The two envelopes paradox*)
Assume that a number 2^n is chosen with probability $2^n / 3^{n+1}$ and the amounts of money 2^n, 2^{n+1} are put into two envelopes. One envelope is chosen randomly and given to you, and the other is given to your friend. Whatever the amount of money in your envelope, the expected amount in your friend's envelope is larger (verify it). Thus, it is worthwhile for you to switch envelopes with him even without opening the envelope! What do you think about this paradoxical conclusion?

Social Choice

Aggregation of Preference Relations

When a rational decision maker forms a preference relation, it is often on the basis of more primitive relations. For example, the choice of a PC may depend on considerations such as "size of memory", "ranking by PC magazine", and "price". Each of these considerations expresses a preference relation on the set of PCs. In this lecture we look at some of the logical properties and problems that arise in the formation of preferences on the basis of more primitive preference relations.

Although the aggregation of preference relations can be thought of in a context of a single individual's decision making, the classic context in which preference aggregation is discussed is "social choice", where the "will of the people" is thought of as an aggregation of the preference relations held by members of society.

The foundations of social choice theory lie in the "Paradox of Voting". Let $X = \{a, b, c\}$ be a set of alternatives. Consider a society that consists of three members called 1, 2, and 3. Their rankings of X are $a \succ_1 b \succ_1 c$, $b \succ_2 c \succ_2 a$, and $c \succ_3 a \succ_3 b$. A natural criterion for the determination of collective opinion on the basis of individuals' preference relations is the *majority rule*. According to the majority rule, $a \succ b$, $b \succ c$, and $c \succ a$, which conflicts with the transitivity of the social preferences. Note that although the majority rule does not induce a transitive social relation for *all* profiles of individuals' preference relations, transitivity might be obtained when we restrict ourselves to a smaller domain of profiles (see problem 3 in the problem set).

The interest in social choice in economics is motivated by the recognition that explicit methods for the aggregation of preference relations are essential for doing any *welfare economics*. Social choice theory is also related to the design of *voting systems*, which are methods for determining social action on the basis of individuals' preferences.

The Basic Model

A basic model of social choice consists of the following:

- X: a set of social *alternatives*.
- N: a finite set of *individuals* (denote the number of elements in N by n).
- $\succ_i$: individual i's ordering on X (an ordering is a preference relation with no indifferences, i.e., for no $x \neq y$, $x \sim_i y$).
- *Profile*: An n-tuple of orderings $(\succ_1, \ldots, \succ_n)$ interpreted as a certain "state of society".
- *SWF (Social Welfare Function)*: A function that assigns a single (social) preference relation (*not* necessarily an ordering) to every profile.

Note that

1. The assumption that the domain of an SWF includes only strict preferences is made only for simplicity of presentation.
2. An SWF attaches a preference relation to *every* possible profile and not just to a single profile.
3. The SWF is required to produce a complete preference relation. An alternative concept, called Social Choice Function, attaches a social alternative, interpreted as the society's choice, to every profile of preference relations.
4. An SWF aggregates only ordinal preference relations. The framework does not allow us to make a statement, relevant in life for determining social preferences, such as "the society prefers a to b since agent 1 prefers b to a but agent 2 prefers a to b much more".
5. In this model we cannot express a consideration of the type "I prefer what society prefers".
6. The elements in X are social alternatives. Thus, an individual's preferences may exhibit considerations of fairness and concern about other individuals' well-being.

Example:

Let us consider some examples of aggregation procedures.

1. $F(\succ_1, \ldots, \succ_n) = \succsim^*$ for some preference relation $\succsim^*$. (This is a degenerate SWF that does not account for the individuals' preferences.)
2. Define $x \rightarrow z$ if a majority of individuals prefer x to z. Order the alternatives by the number of "victories" they score, that is, x is socially preferred to y if $|\{z|x \rightarrow z\}| \geq |\{z|y \rightarrow z\}|$.

3. For $X = \{a, b\}$, $a \succsim b$ unless 2/3 of the individuals prefer b to a.

4. *"The anti-dictator"*: There is an individual i so that x is preferred to y if and only if $y \succ_i x$.

5. Define $d(\succ; \succ_1, \ldots, \succ_n)$ as the number of (x, y, i) for which $x \succ_i y$ and $y \succ x$. The function d can be interpreted as the sum of the distances between the preference relation $\succ$ and the n preference relations of the individuals. Choose $F(\succ_1, \ldots, \succ_n)$ to be an ordering that minimizes $d(\succ; \succ_1, \ldots, \succ_n)$ (ties are broken arbitrarily).

6. Let $F(\succ_1, \ldots, \succ_n)$ be the ordering that is the most common among $(\succ_1, \ldots, \succ_n)$ (with ties broken in some predetermined way).

Axioms

Once again we use the axiomatization methodology. We suggest a set of, hopefully sound, axioms on social welfare functions and study their implications.

Let F be an SWF. We often use $\succsim$ as a short form of $F(\succ_1, \ldots, \succ_n)$.

Condition Par (Pareto):

For all $x, y \in X$ and for every profile $(\succ_i)_{i \in N}$, if $x \succ_i y$ for all i, then $x \succ y$.

The Pareto axiom requires that if all individuals prefer one alternative over the other, then the social preferences agree with the individuals'.

Condition IIA (Independence of Irrelevant Alternatives):

For any pair $x, y \in X$ and any two profiles $(\succ_i)_{i \in N}$ and $(\succ'_i)_{i \in N}$ if for all i, $x \succ_i y$ iff $x \succ'_i y$, then $x \succsim y$ iff $x \succsim' y$.

The IIA condition requires that if two profiles agree on the relative rankings of two particular alternatives, then the social preferences attached to the two profiles also agree in their relative ranking of the two alternatives.

Notice that IIA allows an SWF to apply one criterion when comparing a to b and another when comparing c to d. For example, the simple social preference between a and b can be determined according to majority rule whereas that between c and d requires a 2/3 majority.

Condition IIA is sufficient for Arrow's theorem. However, for the sake of simplifying the proof in this presentation, we will make do with a stronger requirement:

Condition I^* (Independence of Irrelevant Alternatives + Neutrality):
For all $a, b, c, d \in X$, and for any two profiles $(\succ_i)_{i \in N}$ and $(\succ'_i)_{i \in N}$,
if for all i, $a \succ_i b$ iff $c \succ'_i d$, then $a \succsim b$ iff $c \succsim' d$.

In other words, in addition to what is required by IIA, condition I^* requires that the criterion that determines the social preference between a and b be applied to *any* pair of alternatives.

Arrow's Impossibility Theorem

Theorem (Arrow):
If $|X| \geq 3$, then any SWF F that satisfies conditions Par and I^* is dictatorial, that is, there is some i^* such that $F(\succ_1, \ldots, \succ_n) \equiv \succ_{i^*}$.

We can break the theorem's assumptions into four: Par, I^*, *Transitivity* (of the social preferences), and $|X| \geq 3$. Before we move on to the proof, let us show that the assumptions are *independent*. Namely, for each of the four assumptions, we give an example of a nondictatorial SWF, demonstrating the theorem would not hold if that assumption were omitted.

- *Par*: An anti-dictator SWF satisfies I^* but not Par.
- *I^**: Consider the Borda rule. Let $w(1) > w(2) > \ldots > w(|X|)$ be a fixed profile of weights. Say that i assigns to x the score $w(k)$ if x appears in the k'th place in $\succ_i$. Attach to x the sum of the weights assigned to x by the n individuals and rank the alternatives by those sums. The Borda rule is an SWF satisfying Par but not I^*.
- *Transitivity of the Social Order:* The majority rule satisfies all assumptions but can induce a relation that is not transitive.
- $|X| \geq 3$: For $|X| = 2$ the majority rule satisfies Par and I^* and induces (a trivial) transitive relation.

Proof of Arrow's Impossibility Theorem

Let F be an SWF that satisfies Par and I^*. Hereinafter, we write $\succsim$ instead of $F(\succ_1, \ldots, \succ_n)$.

Given the SWF we say that

- a coalition G is *decisive* if for all x,y, [for all $i \in G$, $x \succ_i y$] implies $[x \succ y]$, and

- a coalition G is *almost decisive* if for all x,y, [for all $i \in G$, $x \succ_i y$ and for all $j \notin G$ $y \succ_j x$] implies [$x \succ y$].

Note that if G is decisive it is almost decisive since the "almost decisiveness" refers only to the subset of profiles where all members of G prefer x to y and all members of $N - G$ prefer y to x.

Field Expansion Lemma:

If G is almost decisive, then G is decisive.

Proof:

Consider a profile $(\succ_1, \ldots, \succ_n)$ and a pair of alternatives a, b such that $a \succ_i b$ for all $i \in G$.

Let c be a third alternative. Consider any other profile $(\succ_1^*, \ldots, \succ_n^*)$ satisfying:

- for any $i \in G$: $a \succ_i^* c \succ_i^* b$.
- for any $i \in N - G$ for whom $b \succ_i a$: $c \succ_i^* b \succ_i^* a$.
- for any $i \in N - G$ for whom $a \succ_i b$: $c \succ_i^* a \succ_i^* b$.

Let $F(\succ_1, \ldots, \succ_n) = \succ$ and $F(\succ_1^*, \ldots, \succ_n^*) = \succ^*$.

Since G is almost decisive, $a \succ^* c$. By *Par*, $c \succ^* b$. By transitivity $a \succ^* b$. By I^* (actually we use here only condition I) also $a \succ b$.

Group Contraction Lemma:

If G is decisive and $|G| \geq 2$, then there exists $G' \subset G$ such that G' is decisive.

Proof:

Let $G = G_1 \cup G_2$, where G_1 and G_2 are nonempty and $G_1 \cap G_2 = \emptyset$. By the Field Expansion Lemma it is enough to show that G_1 or G_2 is almost decisive.

Take three alternatives a, b, and c and a profile of preference relations $(\succ_i)_{i \in N}$ satisfying

- for all $i \in G_1$, $c \succ_i a \succ_i b$, and
- for all $i \in G_2$, $a \succ_i b \succ_i c$, and
- for all other i, $b \succ_i c \succ_i a$.

If G_1 is not almost decisive, then there are x and y and a profile $(\succ_i')_{i \in N}$ such that $x \succ_i' y$ for all $i \in G_1$ and $y \succ_i' x$ for all $i \notin G_1$, such that $F(\succ_1', \ldots, \succ_n')$ determines y to be at least as preferable as x. Therefore, by I^*, $b \succsim c$.

Similarly, if G_2 is not almost decisive, then $c \succsim a$. Thus, by transitivity $b \succsim a$, but since G is decisive, $a \succ b$, a contradiction. Thus, G_1 or G_2 is almost decisive.

Proof of the Theorem:

By *Par*, the set N is decisive. By the Group Contraction Lemma, every decisive set that includes more than one member has a proper subset that is decisive. Thus, there is a set $\{i^*\}$ that is decisive, which means that $F(\succ_1, \ldots, \succ_n) \equiv \succ_{i^*}$.

Comment:

Proving the theorem with conditions Par and IIA requires only a few more steps. First, for every two alternatives x and y, define the notion "G is decisive with regard to (x, y)" and "G is almost decisive with regard to (x, y)". Then, proceed through the following steps:

- If G is almost decisive with regard to (x, y), then G is almost decisive with regard to (x, z). (Consider the profile in which for every $i \in G$, $x \succ_i y \succ_i z$, and for every $i \notin G$, $y \succ_i z \succ_i x$.)
- If G is almost decisive with regard to (x, y) then G is almost decisive with regard to (z, y). (Consider the profile in which for every $i \in G$, $z \succ_i x \succ_i y$, and for every $i \notin G$, $y \succ_i z \succ_i x$.)
- If G is almost decisive with regard to (x, y), then G is decisive with regard to (x, y).
- If G is decisive with regard to (x, y) and $|G| \geq 2$, then there exists $G' \subset G$ that is decisive with regard to (x, y).
- For every x and y, there is an individual $i(x, y)$ such that $\{i(x, y)\}$ is decisive with regard to (x, y).
  (The proof of the last three steps is very similar to that given above.)
- Verify that $i(x, y) = i(x', y')$ for every (x, y) and (x', y').

Related Issues

Arrow's theorem was the starting point for a huge literature. We mention three other impossibility results.

1. *Monotonicity* is another axiom that has been widely discussed in the literature. Consider a "change" in a profile so that an alternative a, which individual i ranked below b, is now ranked by i above b. Monotonicity requires that there is no alternative c such that

this change deteriorates the ranking of a vs. c. Muller and Satterthwaite (1977)'s theorem shows that the only SWF's satisfying *Par* and monotonicity are dictatorships.

2. An SWF specifies a preference relation for every profile. A *social choice function* attaches an alternative to every profile. The most striking theorem proved in this framework is the Gibbard-Satterthwaite theorem. It states that any social choice function C satisfying the condition that it is never worthwhile for an individual to misrepresent his preferences, namely, it is never that $C(\succ_1, \ldots, \succ_i', \ldots, \succ_n) \succ_i C(\succ_1, \ldots, \succ_i, \ldots, \succ_n)$, is a dictatorship.

3. Another related concept is the following.

Let $Ch(\succ_1, \ldots, \succ_n)$ be a function that assigns a choice function to every profile of orderings on X. We say that Ch satisfies *unanimity* if for every $(\succ_1, \ldots, \succ_n)$ and for any $x, y \in A$, if $y \succ_i x$ for all i, then $x \neq Ch(\succ_1, \ldots, \succ_n)(A)$.

We say that Ch is *invariant to the procedure* if, for every profile $(\succ_1, \ldots, \succ_n)$ and for every choice set A, the following two "approaches" lead to the same outcome:

a. Partition A into two sets A' and A''. Choose an element from A' and an element from A'' and then choose one element from the two choices.

b. Choose an element from the unpartitioned set A.

Dutta, Jackson, and Le Breton (2001) show that only dictatorships satisfy both unanimity and invariance to the procedure.

Bibliographic Notes

Recommended readings. Kreps 1990, chapter 5; Mas-Colell et al. 1995, chapter 21.

This lecture focuses mainly on Arrow's Impossibility Theorem, one of the most famous results in economics, proved by Arrow in his Ph.D. dissertation and published in 1951 (see the classic book Arrow (1963)). Social choice theory is beautifully introduced in Sen (1970). The proof brought here is one of many for Arrow's Impossibility Theorem (see Kelly (1988)). Reny (2001) provides an elementary proof that demonstrates the strong logical link between Arrow's theorem and the Gibbard-Satterthwaite theorem.

Problem Set 10

Problem 1. (*Moderately difficult. Based on May (1952).*)
Assume that the set of social alternatives, X, includes only two alternatives. Define a social welfare function to be a function that attaches a preference to any profile of preferences (allow indifference for the SWF and the individuals' preference relations). Consider the following axioms:

- *Anonymity* If σ is a permutation of N and if $p = \{ \succsim_i \}_{i \in N}$ and $p' = \{ \succsim_i' \}_{i \in N}$ are two profiles of preferences on X so that $\succsim_{\sigma(i)}' = \succsim_i$, then $\succsim (p) = \succsim (p')$.
- *Neutrality* For any preference $\succsim_i$ define $(- \succsim_i)$ as the preference satisfying $x(- \succsim_i)y$ iff $y \succsim_i x$. Then,
  $$\succsim (\{- \succsim_i \}_{i \in N}) = - \succsim (\{ \succsim_i \}_{i \in N}).$$
- *Positive Responsiveness* If the profile $\{ \succsim_i' \}_{i \in N}$ is identical to $\{ \succsim_i \}_{i \in N}$ with the exception that for one individual j either $(x \sim_j y$ and $x \succ_j' y)$ or $(y \succ_j x$ and $x \sim_j' y)$ and if $x \succsim y$, then $x \succ' y$.

  a. Interpret the axioms.
  b. Show that the majority rule satisfies all of them.
  c. Prove May's theorem by which the majority rule is the only SWF satisfying the above axioms.
  d. Are the above three axioms independent?

Problem 2. (*Standard*)
Assume that the set of alternatives, X, is the interval $[0, 1]$ and that each individual's preference is *single-peaked*, that is, for each i there is an alternative a_i^* such that if $a_i^* \geq b > c$ or $c > b \geq a_i^*$, then $b \succ_i c$.

Show that for any odd n, if we restrict the domain of preferences to single-peaked preferences, then the majority rule induces a " well-behaved" SWF.

Problem 3. (*Moderately difficult*)
Each of N individuals chooses a single object from among a set X, interpreted as his recommendation for the social action. We are interested in functions that aggregate the individuals' recommendations (*not preferences*, just recommendations!) into a social decision (i.e., $F : X^N \to X$).

Discuss the following axioms:

- *Par*: If all individuals recommend x^*, then the society chooses x^*.
- *I*: If the same individuals support an alternative $x \in X$ in two profiles of recommendations, then x is chosen in one profile if and only if it is chosen in the other.

a. Show that if X includes at least three elements, then the only aggregation method that satisfies P and I is a dictatorship.
b. Show the necessity of the three conditions P, I, and $|X| \geq 3$ for this conclusion.

Problem 4. (*Moderately difficult. Based on Kasher and Rubinstein (1997).*)
Who is an economist? Departments of economics are often sharply divided over this question. Investigate the approach according to which the determination of who is an economist is treated as an aggregation of the views held by department members on this question.

Let $N = \{1, \ldots, n\}$ be a group of individuals ($n \geq 3$). Each $i \in N$ "submits" a set E_i, a *proper* nonempty subset of N, which is interpreted as the set of "real economists" in his view. An aggregation method F is a function that assigns a *proper* nonempty subset of N to each profile $(E_i)_{i=1,\ldots,n}$ of proper subsets of N. $F(E_1, \ldots, E_n)$ is interpreted as the set of all members of N who are considered by the group to be economists. (Note that we require that all opinions be proper subsets of N.)

Consider the following axioms on F:

- *Consensus:* If $j \in E_i$ for all $i \in N$, then $j \in F(E_1, \ldots E_n)$, and if $j \notin E_i$ for all $i \in N$, then $j \notin F(E_1, \ldots E_n)$.
- *Independence:* If $(E_1, \ldots, E_L)$ and $(G_1, \ldots, G_n)$ are two profiles of views so that for all $i \in N$, $[j \in E_i$ iff $j \in G_i]$, then $[j \in F(E_1, \ldots, E_n)$ iff $j \in F(G_1, \ldots, G_n)]$.

a. Interpret the two axioms.
b. Find one aggregation method that satisfies Consensus but not Independence and one that satisfies Independence but not Consensus.
c. (*Difficult*) Provide a proof similar to that of Arrow's Impossibility Theorem of the claim that the only aggregation methods that satisfy the above two axioms are those for which there is a member i^* such that $F(E_1, \ldots, E_n) \equiv E_{i^*}$.

Review Problems

The following is a collection of problems based on exams I have given at Tel-Aviv, Princeton and New York universities.

A. Choice

Problem A1. (*Princeton 2000. Based on Fishburn and Rubinstein (1982).*)
Let $X = \mathbb{R}^+ \times \{0, 1, 2, \ldots\}$, where (x, t) is interpreted as receiving $\$x$ at time t. A preference relation on X has the following properties:

- There is indifference between receiving $\$0$ at time 0 and receiving 0 at any other time.
- It is better to receive any positive amount of money as soon as possible.
- Money is desirable.
- The preference between (x, t) and $(y, t + 1)$ is independent of t.
- Continuity.

1. Define formally the continuity assumption for this context.
2. Show that the preference relation has a utility representation.
3. Verify that the preference relation represented by the utility function $u(x)\delta^t$ (with $\delta < 1$ and u continuous, increasing and $u(0) = 0$) satisfies the above properties.
4. Formulize a concept "one preference relation is more impatient than another".
5. Discuss the claim that preferences represented by $u_1(x)\delta_1^t$ are more impatient than preferences represented by $u_2(x)\delta_2^t$ if and only if $\delta_1 < \delta_2$.

Problem A2. (*NYU 2005*)
Let X be a finite set containing at least three elements. Let C be a choice correspondence. Consider the following axiom:
 If $A, B \subseteq X$, $B \subseteq A$, and $C(A) \cap B \neq \emptyset$, then $C(B) = C(A) \cap B$.

1. Show that the axiom is equivalent to the existence of a preference relation $\succsim$ such that $C(A) = \{x \in A | x \succsim a \text{ for all } a \in A\}$.

2. Consider a weaker axiom:

   If $A, B \subseteq X$, $B \subseteq A$, and $C(A) \cap B \neq \emptyset$, then $C(B) \subseteq C(A) \cap B$. Is this sufficient for the above equivalence?

Problem A3. (*NYU 2007. Based on Plott (1973).*)

Let X be a set and C be a choice correspondence defined on all non-empty subsets of X. We say that C satisfies Path Independence (PI) if for every two disjoint sets A and B, we have $C(A \cup B) = C(C(A) \cup C(B))$. We say that C satisfies Extension (E) if $x \in A$ and $x \in C(\{x, y\})$ for every $y \in A$ implies that $x \in C(A)$ for all sets A.

1. Interpret PI and E.
2. Show that if C satisfies both PI and E, then there exists a binary relation $\succsim$ that is complete and reflexive and satisfies $x \succ y$, and $y \succ z$ implies $x \succ z$, such that $C(A) = \{x \in A \mid$ for no $y \in A$ is $y \succ x\}$.
3. Give one example of a choice correspondence satisfying PI but not E, and one satisfying E but not PI.

Problem A4. (*NYU 2008. Based on Eliaz, Richter, and Rubinstein (2011).*)

Let X be a (finite) set of alternatives. Given any choice problem A (where $|A| \geq 2$), the decision maker chooses a set $D(A) \subseteq A$ of two alternatives that he wants to examine more carefully before making the final decision.

The following are two properties of D:

A1: If $a \in D(A)$ and $a \in B \subset A$, then $a \in D(B)$.

A2: If $D(A) = \{x, y\}$ and $a \in D(A - \{x\})$ for some a different than x and y, then $a \in D(A - \{y\})$.

Solve the following four exercises. A full proof is required only for the last exercise:

1. Find an example of a D function that satisfies both A1 and A2.
2. Find a function D that satisfies A1 and not A2.
3. Find a function D that satisfies A2 and not A1.
4. Show that for any function D satisfying A1 and A2 there exists an ordering $\succ$ of the elements of X such that $D(A)$ is the set of the two $\succ$- best elements in A.

Problem A5. (*Tel Aviv 2009. Inspired by Mandler, Manzini, and Mariotti (2010).*)

Consider a decision maker who is choosing an alternative from subsets of a finite set X using the following procedure:

Following a fixed list of properties (a checklist), he examines one property at a time and deletes from the set all the alternatives that do not satisfy this property. When only one alternative remains, he chooses it.

1. Show that if this procedure induces a choice function, then it is consistent with the rational man model.
2. Show that any rational decision maker can be described *as if* he follows this procedure.

Problem A6. (*Tel Aviv 2010*)
A decision maker has a preference relation over $\mathbb{R}_+^n$. A vector (x_1, x_2) is interpreted as an income combination where x_i is the dollar amount the decision maker receives at period i. Let P be the set of all preference relations satisfying:

(i) Strong Monotonicity (SM) in x_1 and x_2.
(ii) Present preference (PP): $(x_1 + \varepsilon, x_2 - \varepsilon) \succsim (x_1, x_2)$ for all $\varepsilon > 0$.

Define $(x_1, x_2) D(y_1, y_2)$ if $(x_1, x_2) \succsim (y_1, y_2)$ for all $\succsim \in P$.

1. Interpret the relation D. Is it a preference relation?
2. Is it true that $(1, 4) D(3, 3)$? What about $(3, 3) D(1, 4)$?
3. Find and prove a proposition of the following type: $(x_1, x_2) D(y_1, y_2)$ if and only if [put here a condition on (x_1, x_2) and (y_1, y_2)].

Problem A7. (*Tel Aviv 2003. Based on Gilboa and Schmeidler (1995).*)
An agent must decide whether to do something, Y, or not to do it, N.

A history is a sequence of results for past events in which the agent chose Y; each result is either a success S or a failure F. For example, (S, S, F, F, S) is a history with five events in which the action was carried out. Two of them (events 3 and 4) ended in failure, whereas the rest were successful.

The decision rule D is a function that assigns the decision Y or N to every possible history.

Consider the following properties of decision rules:

A1   After every history that contains only successes, the decision rule will dictate Y, and after every history that contains only failures, the decision rule will dictate N.

A2   If the decision rule dictates a certain action following some history, it will dictate the same action following any history that is derived from the first history by reordering its members. For example, $D(S, F, S, F, S) = D(S, S, F, F, S)$.

A3 If $D(h) = D(h')$, then this will also be the decision following the concatenation of h and h'. (Reminder: The concatenation of $h = (F, S)$ and $h' = (S, S, F)$ is (F, S, S, S, F)).

1. For every $i = 1, 2, 3$, give an example of a decision rule that does not fulfill property Ai but does fulfill the other two properties.
2. Give an example of a decision rule that fulfills all three properties.
3. (Difficult) Characterize the decision rules that fulfill the three properties.

Problem A8. (*Tel Aviv 2011*)

You have read an article in a "prestigious" journal about a decision maker (DM) whose mental attitude toward elements in a finite set X is represented by a binary relation $\succ$, which is asymmetric and transitive but not necessarily complete. The incompleteness is the result of an assumption that a DM is sometimes unable to compare between alternatives.

Another, presumably stronger, assumption made in the article is that the DM uses the following procedure: he has n criteria in mind, each represented by an ordering (asymmetric, transitive, and complete) $\succ_i$ $(i = 1, \ldots, n)$. The DM decides that $x \succ y$ if and only if $x \succ_i y$ for every i.

1. Verify that the relation $\succ$ generated by this procedure is asymmetric and transitive. Try to convince a reader of the paper that this is an attractive assumption by giving a "real life" example in which it is "reasonable" to assume that a DM uses such a procedure in order to compare between alternatives.

It can be claimed that the additional assumption regarding the procedure that generates $\succ$ is not a "serious" one since given any asymmetric and transitive relation, $\succ$, one can find a set of complete orderings $\succ_1, \ldots, \succ_n$ such that $x \succ y$ iff $x \succ_i y$ for every i.

2. Demonstrate this claim for the relation on the set $X = \{a, b, c\}$ according to which only $a \succ b$ and the comparison between [b and c] and [a and c] are not determined.
3. (Main part of the question) Prove this claim for the general case. Guidance (for c): given an asymmetric and transitive relation $\succ$ on an arbitrary X, define a set of complete orderings $\{\succ_i\}$ and prove that $x \succ y$ iff for every i, $x \succ_i y$.

B. The Consumer and the Producer

Problem B1. (*Princeton 2002*)
Consider a consumer with a preference relation in a world with two goods, X (an aggregated consumption good) and M ("membership in a club", for example), which can be consumed or not. In other words, the consumption of X can be any nonnegative real number, while the consumption of M must be either 0 or 1.

Assume that the consumer's preferences are strictly monotonic and continuous and satisfy the following property:

> *Property E*: For every x, there is y such that $(y, 0) \succ (x, 1)$ (i.e., there is always some amount of the aggregated consumption good that can compensate for the loss of membership).

1. Show that any consumer's preference relation can be represented by a utility function of the type:

$$u(x, m) = \begin{cases} x & if \quad m = 0 \\ x + g(x) & if \quad m = 1 \end{cases}.$$

2. (Less easy) Show that the consumer's preference relation can also be represented by a utility function of the type:

$$u(x, m) = \begin{cases} f(x) & if \quad m = 0 \\ f(x) + v & if \quad m = 1 \end{cases}.$$

3. Explain why continuity and strong monotonicity (without property E) are not sufficient for (1).
4. Calculate the consumer's demand function.
5. Taking the utility function to be of the form described in (1), derive the consumer's indirect utility function. For the case where the function g is differentiable, verify Roy's identity with respect to commodity M.

Problem B2. (*Princeton 2001*)

1. Define a formal concept for "$\succsim_1$ and $\succsim_0$ are closer than $\succsim_2$ and $\succsim_0$".
2. Apply your definition to the class of preference relations represented by $U_1 = tU_2 + (1 - t)U_0$, where the function U_i represents $\succsim_i$ ($i = 0, 1, 2$).
3. Consider the above definition in the consumer context. Denote by $x_k^i(p, w)$ the demand function of $\succsim_i$ for good k. Show that $\succsim_1$ and

$\succsim_0$ may be closer than $\succsim_2$ and $\succsim_0$, and nevertheless $|x_k^1(p, w) - x_k^0(p, w)| > |x_k^2(p, w) - x_k^0(p, w)|$ for some commodity k, price vector p and wealth level w.

Problem B3. (*Tel Aviv 2003*)

Consider the following consumer problem: there are two goods, 1 and 2. The consumer has a certain endowment. His preferences satisfy monotonicity and continuity. Before the consumer are two "exchange functions": he can exchange x units of good 1 for $f(x)$ units of good 2, or he can exchange y units of good 2 for $g(y)$ units of good 1. Assume the consumer can make only one exchange.

1. Show that if the exchange functions are continuous, then a solution to the consumer problem exists.
2. Explain why strong convexity of the preference relation is not sufficient to guarantee a unique solution if the functions f and g are increasing and convex.
3. Interpret the statement "the function f is increasing and convex".
4. Suppose both functions f and g are differentiable and concave and that the product of their derivatives at point 0 is 1. Suppose also that the preference relation is strongly convex. Show that under these conditions, the agent will not find two different exchanges, one exchanging good 1 for good 2, and one exchanging good 2 for good 1, optimal.
5. Now assume $f(x) = ax$ and $g(y) = by$. Explain this assumption. Find a condition that will ensure it is not profitable for the consumer to make more than one exchange.

Problem B4. (*Tel Aviv 1998*)

A consumer with wealth $w = 10$ "must" obtain a book from one of three stores. Denote the prices at each store as p_1, p_2, p_3. All prices are below w in the relevant range. The consumer has devised a strategy: he compares the prices at the first two stores and purchases the book from the first store if its price is not greater than the price at the second store. If $p_1 > p_2$, he compares the prices of the second and third stores and purchases the book from the second store if its price is not greater than the price at the third store. He uses the remainder of his wealth to purchase other goods.

1. What is this consumer's "demand function"?
2. Does this consumer satisfy "rational man" assumptions?

3. Consider the function $v(p_1, p_2, p_3) = w - p_{i^*}$, where i^* is the store from which the consumer purchases the book if the prices are (p_1, p_2, p_3). What does this function represent?

4. Explain why $v(\cdot)$ is not monotonically decreasing in p_i. Compare with the indirect utility function of the classic consumer model.

Problem B5. (*NYU 2005*)

A consumer has preferences that satisfy monotonicity, continuity, and strict convexity, in a world of K goods. The goods are split into two categories, 1 and 2, of K_1 and K_2 goods respectively ($K_1 + K_2 = K$). The consumer receives two types of money: w_i units of money of type i, which can be exchanged only for goods in the i'th category given a price vector p_i.

Define the induced preference relation over the two-dimensional space (w_1, w_2). Show that these preferences are monotonic, continuous, and convex.

Problem B6. (*NYU 2006*)

Consider a consumer in a world of 2 commodities who has to make choices from budget sets parametrized by (p, w), with the additional constraint that the consumption of good 1 is limited by some external bound $c \geq 0$. That is, in his world, a choice problem is a set of the form $B(p, w, c) = \{x | px \leq w \text{ and } x_1 \leq c\}$. Denote by $x(p, w, c)$ the consumer's choice from $B(p, w, c)$.

1. Assume that $px(p, w, c) = w$ and $x_1(p, w, c) = \min\{0.5w/p_1, c\}$. Show that this behavior is consistent with the assumption that demand is derived from a maximization of some preference relation.

2. Assume that $px(p, w, c) = w$ and $x_1(p, w, c) = \min\{0.5c, w/p_1\}$. Show that this consumer's behavior is inconsistent with preference maximization.

3. Assume that the consumer chooses his demand for x by maximizing the utility function $u(x)$. Denote the indirect utility by $V(p, w, c) = u(x(p, w, c))$. Assume V is "well-behaved". Outline the idea of how one can derive the demand function from the function V in case that $\partial V / \partial c(p, w, c) > 0$.

Problem B7. (*Tel Aviv 2006*)

Imagine a consumer who lives in a world with $K + 1$ commodities and behaves in the following manner: The consumer is characterized by a vector D, consisting of the commodities $1, \ldots, K$. If he can purchase D, he will consume it and spend the rest of his income on commodity $K + 1$. If he is unable to purchase D, he will not consume commodity $K + 1$ and will purchase the bundle tD ($t \leq 1$) where t is as large as he can afford.

1. Show that there exists a monotonic and convex preference relation that explains this pattern of behavior.
2. Show that there is no monotonic and continuous preference relation that explains this pattern of behavior.

Problem B8. (*NYU 2007*)

A consumer in a world of K commodities maximizes the utility function $u(x) = \sum_k x_k^2$.

1. Calculate the consumer's demand function (whenever it is uniquely defined).
2. Give another preference relation (not just a monotonic transformation of u) that induces the same demand function.
3. For the original utility function u, calculate the indirect preferences for $K = 2$. What is the relationship between the indirect preferences and the demand function? (It is sufficient to answer for the domain where $p_1 < p_2$.)
4. Are the preferences in (1) differentiable (according to the definition given in class)?

Problem B9. (*NYU 2008*)

A decision maker has a preference relation over the pairs (x_{me}, x_{him}) with the interpretation that x_{me} is an amount of money he will get and x_{him} is the amount of money another person will get. Assume that:

(*i*)   for all (a, b) such that $a > b$, the decision maker strictly prefers (a, b) over (b, a).

(*ii*)   if $a' > a$, then $(a', b) \succ (a, b)$.

The decision maker has to allocate M between him and another person.

1. Show that these assumptions guarantee that he will never allocate to the other person more than he gives himself.
2. Assume (*i*), (*ii*), and
   (*iii*) The decision maker is indifferent between (a, a) and $(a - \epsilon, a + 4\epsilon)$ for all a and $\epsilon > 0$.
   Show that nevertheless he might allocate the money equally.

3. Assume (i), (ii), (iii), and

   (iv) The decision maker's preferences are also differentiable (according to the definition given in class).

   Show that in this case, he will allocate to himself (strictly) more than to the other.

Problem B10. (*NYU 2009*)

An economic agent is both a producer and a consumer. He has a_0 units of good 1. He can use some of a_0 to produce commodity 2. His production function f satisfies monotonicity, continuity, and strict concavity. His preferences satisfy monotonicity, continuity, and convexity. Given he uses a units of commodity 1 in production, he is able to consume the bundle $(a_0 - a, f(a))$ for $a \leq a_0$. The agent has in his "mind" three "centers":

- The *pricing center* declares a price vector (p_1, p_2).
- The *production center* takes the price vector as given and operates according to one of the following two rules:

  Rule 1:   maximizing profits, $p_2 f(a) - p_1 a$.
  Rule 2:   maximizing production subject to the constraint of not making any losses, that is, $p_2 f(a) - p_1 a \geq 0$.

  The output of the production center is a consumption bundle.
- The *consumption center* takes $(a_0 - a, f(a))$ as endowment and finds the optimal consumption allocation that it can afford according to the prices declared by the pricing center.

The prices declared by the pricing center are chosen to create harmony between the other two centers in the sense that the consumption center finds the outcome of the production center's activity, $(a_0 - a, f(a))$, optimal given the announced prices.

1. Show that under Rule 1, the economic agent consumes the bundle $(a_0 - a*, f(a*))$ which maximizes his preferences.
2. What is the economic agent's consumption with Rule 2?
3. State and prove a general conclusion about the comparison between the behavior of two individuals, one whose production center operates with Rule 1 and one whose production center activates Rule 2.

Problem B11. (*Tel Aviv 2010*)

A basketball coach considers buying players from a set A. Given a budget w and a price vector $(p_a)_{a \in A}$, the coach can purchase any set such that the total cost of the players in it is not greater than w. Discuss the rationality of each of the following choice procedures, defined for any budget level w and price vector P:

(P1) The consumer has in mind a fixed list of the players in A: $a_1, \ldots, a_n$. Starting at the beginning of the list, when he arrives to the $i'th$ player, he adds him to the team if his budget allows him to after his past decisions and then continues to the next player on the list with his remaining budget. This continues until he runs out of budget or has gone through the entire list.

(P2) He purchases the combination of players that minimize the excess budget he is left with.

Problem B12. (*Tel Aviv 2011*)

A consumer in a two-commodity world operates in the following manner: The consumer has a preference relation $\succsim_S$ on $\mathbb{R}^2_+$. His father has a preference relation $\succsim_F$ on the space of his son's consumption bundles. Both relations satisfy strong monotonicity, continuity, and strict convexity. The father does not allow his son to purchase a bundle that is not as good (from his perspective) as the bundle $(M, 0)$. The son, when choosing from a budget set, maximizes his own preferences subject to the constraint imposed by his father. In the case that he cannot satisfy his father's wishes, he feels free to maximize his own preferences.

1. Prove that the behavior of the son is rationalizable.
2. Prove that the preferences that rationalize this kind of behavior are monotonic.
3. Show that the preferences that rationalize this kind of behavior are not necessarily continuous or convex (you can demonstrate this diagrammatically).
4. (Bonus) Assume that the father's instructions are that given the budget set (p, w) the son is not to purchase any bundle that is $\succsim_F$-worse than $(w/p_1, 0)$. The son seeks to maximize his preferences subject to satisfying his father's wishes. Show that the son's behavior satisfies the Weak Axiom of Revealed Preferences.

Problem B13. (*NYU 2005, inspired by Chen, Lakshminarayanan, and Santos (2005)*.)

In an experiment, a monkey is given $m = 12$ coins, which he can exchange for apples or bananas. The monkey faces m consecutive choices in which he gives a coin either to an experimenter holding a apples or another experimenter holding b bananas.

1. Assume that the experiment is repeated with different values of a and b and that each time the monkey trades the first 4 coins for apples and the next 8 coins for bananas.

   Show that the monkey's behavior is consistent with the classical assumptions of consumer behavior (namely, that his behavior can be explained as the maximization of a monotonic, continuous, and convex preference relation on the space of bundles).

2. Assume that it was later observed that when the monkey holds an arbitrary number m of coins, then, irrespective of the values of a and b, he exchanges the first 4 coins for apples and the remaining $m - 4$ coins for bananas. Is this behavior consistent with the rational consumer model?

C. Uncertainty

Problem C1. (*Princeton 2001*)

A consumer has to make a choice of a bundle *before* he is informed whether a certain event, which is expected with probability α and affects his welfare, has happened or not. He assigns a vNM utility $v(x)$ to the consumption of the bundle x when the event occurs, and a vNM utility $v'(x)$ to the consumption of x should the event not occur. Having to choose a bundle, the consumer maximizes his expected utility $\alpha v(x) + (1 - \alpha)v'(x)$. Both v and v' induce preferences on the set of bundles satisfying the standard assumptions about the consumer. Assume also that v and v' are concave.

1. Show that the consumer's preference relation is convex.
2. Find a connection between the consumer's indirect utility function and the indirect utility functions derived from v and v'.
3. A new commodity appears on the market: "A discrete piece of information that tells the consumer whether or not the event occurred". The commodity can be purchased prior to the consumption decision. Use the indirect utility functions to characterize the demand function for the new commodity.

Problem C2. (*Tel Aviv 1999*)

Tversky and Kahneman (1986) report the following experiment: each participant receives a questionnaire asking him to make two choices, the first from $\{a, b\}$ and the second from $\{c, d\}$:

a. A sure profit of \$240.
b. A lottery between a profit of \$1,000 with probability 25% and 0 with probability 75%.

   c. A sure loss of $750.

   d. A lottery between a loss of $1,000 with probability 75% and 0 with probability 25%.

The participant will receive the sum of the outcomes of the two lotteries he chooses. 73% of the participants chose the combination a and d. Is their behavior sensible?

Problem C3. (*NYU 2007*)
Identify a professor's lifetime with the interval $[0, 1]$. There are $K + 1$ academic ranks, $0, \ldots, K$. All professors start at rank 0 and eventually reach rank K. Define a career as a sequence $t = (t_1, \ldots, t_K)$ where $t_0 = 0 \le t_1 \le t_2 \le \ldots \le t_K \le 1$ with the interpretation that t_k is the time it takes to get the k'th promotion. (Note that a professor can receive multiple promotions at the same time.) Denote by $\succsim$ the professor's preferences on the set of all possible careers.

   For any $\epsilon > 0$ and for any career t such that $t_K \le 1 - \epsilon$, define $t + \epsilon$ to be the career $(t + \epsilon)_k = t_k + \epsilon$ (i.e., all promotions are delayed by ϵ).

   Following are two properties of the professor's preferences:

Monotonicity: For any two careers t and s, if $t_k \le s_k$ for all k, then $t \succsim s$, and if $t_k < s_k$ for all k, then $t \succ s$.

Invariance: For every $\epsilon > 0$ and every two careers t and s for which $t + \epsilon$ and $s + \epsilon$ are well defined, $t \succsim s$ iff $t + \epsilon \succsim s + \epsilon$.

1. Formulate the set L of careers in which a professor receives all K promotions at the same time. Show that if $\succsim$ satisfies continuity and monotonicity, then for every career t there is a career $s \in L$ such that $s \sim t$.

2. Show that any preference that is represented by the function $U(t) = -\sum \Delta_k t_k$ (for some $\Delta_k > 0$) satisfies Monotonicity, Invariance, and Continuity.

3. One professor evaluates a career by the maximum length of time one has to wait for a promotion, and the smaller this number the better. Show that these preferences cannot be represented by the utility function described in (2).

Problem C4. (*NYU 2008*)
An economic agent has to choose between projects. The outcome of each project is uncertain. It might yield a failure or one of K "types of success". Thus, each project z can be described by a vector of K

non-negative numbers, $(z_1, \ldots, z_K)$, where z_k stands for the probability that the project success will be of type k. Let $Z \subset \mathbb{R}_+^K$ be the set of feasible projects. Assume Z is compact and convex and satisfies "free disposal". The decision maker is an Expected Utility maximizer. Denote by u_k the vNM utility from the k'th type of success, and attach 0 to failure. Thus the decision maker chooses a project (vector) $z \in Z$ in order to maximize $\sum z_k u_k$.

1. First, formalize the decision maker's problem. Then, formalize (and prove) the claim: if the decision maker suddenly values type k success higher than before, he would choose a project assigning a higher probability to k.

2. Apparently, the decision maker realizes that there is an additional uncertainty. The world may go "one way or another". With probability α the vNM utility of the k'th type of success will be u_k and with probability $1 - \alpha$ it will be v_k. Failure remains 0 in both contingencies.

   First, formalize the decision maker's new problem. Then, formalize (and prove) the claim: Even if the decision maker would obtain the same expected utility, would he have known in advance the direction of the world, the existence of uncertainty makes him (at least weakly) less happy.

Problem C5. (*NYU 2009*)

For any nonnegative integer n and a number $p \in [0, 1]$, let (n, p) be the lottery that gets the prize \$$n$ with probability p and \$0 with probability $1 - p$. Let us call those lotteries *simple lotteries*. Consider preference relations on the space of simple lotteries.

We say that such a preference relation satisfies Independence if $p \succeq q$ iff $\alpha p \oplus (1 - \alpha) r \succeq \alpha q \oplus (1 - \alpha) r$ for any $\alpha > 0$, and any simple lotteries p, q, r for which the compound lotteries are also simple lotteries.

Consider a preference relation satisfying the Independence axiom, strictly monotonic in money and continuous in p. Show that:

1. (n, p) is monotonic in p for $n > 0$, that is, for all $p > p'$ $(n, p) \succ (n, p')$.
2. For all n there is a unique $v(n)$ such that $(1, 1) \sim (n, 1/v(n))$.
3. It can be represented with the expected utility formula: that is, there is an increasing function v such that $pv(n)$ is a utility function that represents the preference relation.

Problem C6. (*Princeton 1997*)

A decision maker forms preferences over the set X of all possible distributions of a population over two categories (such as living in two locations). An element in X is a vector (x_1, x_2) where $x_i \geq 0$ and $x_1 + x_2 = 1$. The decision maker has two considerations in mind:

- He thinks that if $x \succsim y$, then for any z, the mixture of $\alpha \in [0, 1]$ of x with $(1 - \alpha)$ of z should be at least as good as the mixture of α of y with $(1 - \alpha)$ of z.
- He is indifferent between a distribution that is fully concentrated in location 1 and one that is fully concentrated in location 2.

1. Show that the only preference relation that is consistent with the two principles is the degenerate indifference relation ($x \sim y$ for any $x, y \in X$).
2. The decision maker claims that you are wrong because his preference relation is represented by a utility function $|x_1 - 1/2|$. Why is he wrong?

Problem C7. (*NYU 2006*)

Consider a world with balls of K different colors. An object is called a bag and is specified by a vector $x = (x_1, .., x_K)$ (where x_k is a nonnegative integer indicating the number of balls of color k). For convenience, denote by $n(x) = \sum x_k$ the number of balls in bag x.

An individual has a preference relation over bags of balls.

1. Suggest a context where it will make sense to assume that:

    i.   For any integer λ, $x \sim \lambda x$.

    ii. If $n(x) = n(y)$, then $x \succsim y$ iff $x + z \succsim y + z$.

2. Show that any preference relation that is represented by $U(x) = \sum x_k v_k / n(x)$ for some vector of numbers $(v_1, \ldots, v_k)$ satisfies the two axioms.
3. Find a preference relation that satisfies the two properties that cannot be represented in the form suggested in (2).

D. Social Choice

Problem D1. (*Princeton 2000*)

Consider the following social choice problem: a group has n members who must choose from a set containing 3 elements $\{A, B, L\}$, where A

and B are prizes and L is the lottery that yields each of the prizes A and B with equal probability. Each member has a strict preference over the three alternatives that satisfies vNM assumptions. Show that there is a nondictatorial social welfare function that satisfies the independence of irrelevant alternatives axiom (even the strict version I^*) and the Pareto axiom (Par). Reconcile this fact with Arrow's Impossibility Theorem.

Problem D2. (*NYU 2009*)
We will say that a choice function C is consistent with the *majority vetoes a dictator procedure* if there are three preference relations $\succ_1$, $\succ_2$, and $\succ_3$ such that $c(A)$ is the $\succ_1$ maximum unless both $\succ_2$ and $\succ_3$ agree on another alternative being the maximum in A.

1. Show that such a choice function might not be rationalizable.
2. Show that such a choice function satisfies the following property: if $c(A) = a$, $c(A - \{b\}) = c$ for b and c different from a, then $c(B) = c$ for any B that contains c and is a subset of $A - \{b\}$.
3. Show that not all choice functions could be explained by the majority vetoes a dictator procedure.

Problem D3. (*Tel Aviv 2009. Inspired by Miller (2007).*)
Lately we have been using the term a "reasonable reaction" quite frequently. In this problem we assume that this term is defined according to the opinions of the individuals in the society with regard to the question: "What is a reasonable reaction?"

Assume that in a certain situation, the possible set of reactions is X and the set of individuals in the society is N.

A "reasonability perception" is a nonempty set of possible reactions that are perceived as reasonable.

The social reasonability perception is determined by a function f that attaches a reasonability perception (a nonempty subset of X) to any profile of the individuals' reasonability perception (a vector of nonempty subsets of X).

1. Formalize the following proposition:
   Assume that the number of reactions in X is larger than the number of individuals in the society and that f satisfies the following four properties:

   a. If in a certain profile all the individuals do not perceive a certain reaction as reasonable, then neither does the society.
   b. All the individuals have the same status.

    c. All the reactions have the same status.

    d. Consider two profiles that are different only in one individual's reasonability perception. Any reaction that f determines to be reasonable in the first profile, and regarding which the individual did not change his opinion from reasonable to unreasonable in the second profile, remains reasonable.

Then f determines that a reaction is socially reasonable if and only if at least one of the individuals perceives it as reasonable.

2. Show that all four properties are necessary for the proposition.
3. Prove the proposition.

Problem D4. (*Tel Aviv 2010*)

Let $\succsim$ be a preference relation on $\mathbb{R}^n$ satisfying the following two properties:

    Weak Pareto (WP): If $x_i \geq y_i$ for all i, then $x = (x_1, \ldots, x_n) \succsim y = (y_1, \ldots, y_n)$, and if $x_i > y_i$ for all i, then $(x_1, \ldots, x_n) \succ (y_1, \ldots, y_n)$.

    Independence (IIA): Let $a, b, c, d \in \mathbb{R}^n$ be vectors such that in any coordinate $a_i > b_i$, $a_i = b_i$, or $a_i < b_i$ if and only if $c_i > d_i$, $c_i = d_i$, or $c_i < d$, accordingly. Then, $a \succsim b$ iff $c \succsim d$.

1. Find a preference relation different from those represented by $u_i(x_1, \ldots, x_n) = x_i$ which satisfies the two properties.
2. Show, for $n = 2$, that there is an i such that $a_i > b_i$ implies $a \succ b$.
3. Provide a "social choice" interpretation for the result in (2). Explain how it differs from Arrow's Impossibility Theorem.
4. Expand (2) for any n.

References

Arrow, K. J. (1963). *Social Choice and Individual Values*. 2d edition. New York: Wiley.

Arrow, K. J. (1970). *Essays in the Theory of Risk Bearing*. Chicago: Markham.

Arrow, K. J., and F. Hahn (1971). *General Competitive Analysis*. San Francisco: Holden-Day.

Bernoulli, D. (1954). "Exposition of a new theory on the measurement of risk." *Econometrica* 22: 23–36.

Bowles, S. (2003) *Microeconomics: Behavior, Institutions, and Evolution*. Princeton, N.J.: Princeton University Press.

Chen, M. K., V. Lakshminarayanan, and L. Santos (2005). "The evolution of our preferences: Evidence from Capuchin-monkey trading behavior." *Journal of Political Economy* 114(3): 517-537.

Cherepanov, V., T. Feddersen, and A. Sandroni (2008). "Rationalization." Working paper, Kellogg School of Management.

Debreu, G. (1954). "Representation of a preference ordering by a numerical function." In *Decision Processes*, ed. R. Thrall, C. Coombs, and R. Davis. New York: Wiley.

Debreu, G. (1959). *Theory of Value*. New York: Wiley.

Debreu, G. (1960). *Mathematical Methods in the Social Sciences*. Stanford, Calif.: Stanford University Press.

Diewert, W. E. (1982). "Duality approaches to microeconomic theory." Chap.12 in *Handbook of Mathematical Economics*, vol. 2, ed. K. Arrow and M. Intriligator. Amsterdam: North-Holland.

Dutta, B., M. O. Jackson, and M. Le Breton (2001). "Strategic candidacy and voting procedures." *Econometrica* 69: 1013–1037.

Eliaz, K., M. Richter, and A. Rubinstein (2011). "Choosing the two finalists." *Economic Theory* 46: 211–219.

Fishburn, P. (1970). *Utility Theory for Decision Making*. New York: Wiley.

Fishburn, P., and A. Rubinstein (1982). "Time preferences." *International Economic Review* 23: 677–694.

Gilboa, I. (2009). *Theory of Decision under Uncertainty*. Cambridge: Cambridge University Press.

Gilboa, I., and D. Schmeidler (1995). "Case-based decision theory." *The Quarterly Journal of Economics* 110: 605–639.

Handa, J. (1977). "Risk, probabilities, and a new theory of cardinal utility." *The Journal of Political Economy* 85: 97–122.

Hicks, J. R. (1939). *Value and Capital: An Inquiry into Some Fundamental Principles of Economic Theory.* Oxford: Oxford University Press.

Hicks, J. R. (1946). *Value and Capital.* Oxford: Clarendon Press.

Hicks, J. R. (1956). *A Revision of Demand Theory.* Oxford: Clarendon Press.

Houthakker, H. S. (1950). "Revealed preference and the utility function." *Economica* 17: 159–174.

Huber, J., J. Payne, and C. Puto (1982). "Adding asymmetrically dominated alternatives: Violations of regularity and the similarity hypothesis." *Journal of Consumer Research* 9: 90–98.

Jehle, G., and P. J. Reny (1997). *Advanced Microeconomic Theory.* Boston: Addison-Wesley.

Kahneman, D. (2000). "Evaluation by moments: Past and future." In *Choices, Values, and Frames*, ed. D. Kahneman and A. Tversky. 693–708. New York: Cambridge University Press.

Kahneman, D., and A. Tversky (1979). "Prospect theory: An analysis of decision under risk." *Econometrica* 47: 263–292.

Kahneman, D., and A. Tversky (1984). "Choices, values, and frames." *American Psychologist* 39: 341–350.

Kahneman, D., and A. Tversky (2000). *Choices, Values, and Frames.* Cambridge, U.K.: Cambridge University Press.

Kalai, G., A. Rubinstein, and R. Spiegler (2002). "Comments on rationalizing choice functions which violate rationality." *Econometrica* 70: 2481–2488.

Kannai, Y., and B. Peleg (1984). "A note on the extension of an order on a set to the power set." *Journal of Economic Theory* 32: 172–175.

Kasher, A., and A. Rubinstein (1997). "On the question 'Who is a J?' ' : A social choice approach." *Logique et Analyse* 160: 385–395.

Kelly, J. S. (1988). *Social Choice Theory: An Introduction.* New York: Springer-Verlag.

Kreps, D. (1988). *Notes on the Theory of Choice.* Boulder, Colo.: Westview Press.

Kreps, D. (1990). *A Course in Microeconomic Theory.* Princeton, N.J.: Princeton University Press.

Luce, Duncan R. (1956). "Semiorders and a theory of utility discrimination." *Econometrica* 24: 178–191.

Luce, D. R., and H. Raiffa. (1957). *Games and Decisions.* New York: Wiley.

Machina, M. (1987). "Choice under uncertainty: Problems solved and unsolved." *Journal of Economic Perspectives* 1: 121–154.

Mandler M., P. Manzini, and M. Mariotti (2010). "A million answers to twenty questions: Choosing by checklist." Working paper.

Markowitz, H. (1959). *Portfolio Selection: Efficient Diversification of Investments*. New York: Wiley.

Mas-Colell, A., M. D. Whinston, and J. R. Green (1995). *Microeconomic Theory*. Oxford: Oxford University Press.

Masatlioglu, Y., and E. A. Ok (2005). "Rational choice with status-quo bias." *Journal of Economic Theory* 121: 1–29.

May, O. (1952). "A set of independent necessary and sufficient conditions for simple majority decision." *Econometrica* 20: 680–684.

McKenzie, L. (1957). "Demand theory without a utility index." *Review of Economic Studies 24*: 185–189.

Miller, A.D. (2007). "A model of community standards." Working paper.

Miyamoto, J. M., P. P. Wakker, H. Bleichrodt, and H. J. M. Peters (1998). "The zero-condition: A simplifying assumption in QALY measurement and multi-attribute utility." *Management Science* 44: 839–849.

Muller, E., and M. A. Satterthwaite (1977). "The equivalence of strong positive association and strategy proofness." *Journal of Economic Theory* 14: 412–418.

Plott, C. E. (1973). "Path independence, rationality, and social choice." *Econometrica* 41: 1075–1091.

Pratt, J. (1964). "Risk aversion in the small and in the large." *Econometrica* 32: 122–136.

Rabin, M. (1998). "Psychology and economics." *Journal of Economic Literature* 36: 11–46.

Rabin, M. (2000). "Risk aversion and expected-utility theory: A calibration theorem." *Econometrica* 68: 1281–1292.

Radner, R. (1993). "The organization of decentralized information processing." *Econometrica* 61: 1109–1146.

Reny, P. J. (2001). "Arrow's theorem and the Gibbard-Satterthwaite theorem: A unified approach." *Economic Letters* 70: 99–105.

Richter, M. K. (1966). "Revealed preference theory." *Econometrica* 34: 635–645.

Rothschild, M., and J. Stiglitz (1970). "Increasing risk I: A definition." *Journal of Economic Theory* 2: 225–243.

Roy, R. (1942). *De l'utilité*. Paris: Hermann.

Rubinstein, A. (1988). "Similarity and decision-making under risk." *Journal of Economic Theory* 46: 145–153.

Rubinstein, A. (1998). *Modeling Bounded Rationality*. Boston: MIT Press.

Rubinstein, A. (2002). "Irrational diversification in multiple decision problems." *European Economic Review* 46: 1369–1378.

Rubinstein, A. (2006). "Dilemmas of an economic theorist." *Econometrica* 74: 865–883.

Rubinstein, A., and Y. Salant (2006a). "A model of choice from lists." *Theoretical Economics* 1: 3–17.

Rubinstein, A., and Y. Salant (2006b). "Two comments on the principle of revealed preference." Mimeo.

Samuelson, P. A. (1948). "Consumption theory in terms of revealed preference." *Economica* 15: 243–253.

Sen, A. (1970). *Individual Choice and Social Welfare*. San Fransisco: Holden-Day.

Sen, A. (1993). "Internal consistency of choice." *Econometrica* 61: 495–521.

Shafir, E., I. Simonson, and A. Tversky (1993). "Reason based theory." *Cognition* 49: 11–36.

Simon, H. (1955). "A behavioral model a rational choice." *Quarterly Journal of Economics*, 69: 99–118.

Slovic, P., and S. Lichtenstein (1968). "Relative importance of probabilities and payoffs in risk taking." *Journal of Experimental Psychology Monograph* 78: 1–18.

Tversky, A., and D. Kahneman (1986). "Rational choice and the framing of decisions." *Journal of Business* 59: 261–278.

Tversky, A., and E. Shafir (1992). "Choice under conflict: The dynamics of deferred decision." *Psychological Science* 3: 358–361.

Varian, A. (1984). *Microeconomic Analysis*. 2d edition. New York: Norton.

von Neumann, J., and R. Morgenstern. (1944). *Theory of Games and Economic Behavior*. Princeton, N.J.: Princeton University Press.

Yaari, M. E. (1985). "On the role of 'Dutch Books' in the theory of choice under risk." Nancy Shwartz Memorial Lecture, reprinted in *Frontiers of Research in Economic Theory: The Nancy L. Shwartz Memorial Lectures, 1983–1997* ed. D. P. Jacobs, E. Kalai, M. I. Kamien, N. L. Shwartz, P. Hammond, and A. Holly. New York: Cambridge University Press.

Yaari, M. E. (1987). "The dual theory of choice under risk." *Econometrica* 55: 95–115.

Index